A HISTORY OF
ADDICTION & RECOVERY
IN THE
UNITED STATES

MICHAEL LEMANSKI

SEE SHARP PRESS

Lemanski, Michael.

A history of addiction &
recovery in the United

For information contact See Sharp Press, P.O. Box 1731,
Tucson, AZ 85702-1731.
Web site: http://www.seesharppress.com

Lemanski, Michael.
   A History of addiction & recovery in the United States / Michael
Lemanski ; with an introduction by Jerry Dorsman. — Tucson, Ariz. : See
Sharp Press, 2001.
      154 p. ; 23 cm.
      Includes bibliographical references and index.
      ISBN 1-884365-26-4

      1. Alcoholism—Treatment—United States—History.
   2. Alcoholics—Rehabilitation—United States—History.
   3. Alcoholics Anonymous—History. 4. Twelve-step programs—History.
   5. Substance abuse—Treatment—United States—History. I. Title.

                          362.29180973

First Printing

Printed in USA with soy-based ink on acid-free paper by Thomson-Shore, Inc.

Contents

Introduction

What helps individuals break an addiction to alcohol? What works? Recent Gallup polls, independent polls, and epidemiological studies indicate that 30 to 33 million Americans have had some kind of drinking problem. One of these studies by two senior executives at the research firm J. Walter Thompson produced additional data. This study revealed that of 30 million present and former problem drinkers, 11 million were still drinking abusively and 19 million were not.

What makes this so impressive? Well, we know from AA's internal audits that it has about 1.16 million members in the United States. This means that AA helps about 6% of problem drinkers. Or, to put it the other way, 94% of those who have overcome problems with alcohol don't attend Alcoholics Anonymous.

Yet a mind-blowing 96% of the inpatient treatment facilities in the U.S. are 12-Step facilities, which have AA as their centerpiece. How did our addiction treatment industry get so far off the mark?

For answers, read this book.

Here, Michael Lemanski traces the history of addiction treatment in America. He peels back layer after layer and explains why things are the way they are. He shows that the recovery movement over the past 200 years has been more of a religious than a scientific enterprise.

He follows the path of the early temperance movement, a Christian-based enterprise. He describes "The Washingtonians," a mid-1800s group which had some surprising similarities to modern-day AA. He divulges tactics of the crusaders of the Women's Christian Temperance Union (WCTU). He also recounts the saga of the religious and moral activists who pushed for, and helped to bring about, Prohibition, the U.S. ban on the sale of alcoholic beverages which lasted from 1920 to 1933.

In the early 20th century, not much changed. The ongoing movement to help people who were struggling with alcohol problems remained firmly religious. The Salvation Army emerged with what appeared to be a complete program. This organization offered food and shelter along with "9 steps" to help problem drinkers find a new life. (As you read these 9 steps, take a moment to compare them to AA's 12.) Then there was another Christian program, the Emmanuel Movement, which included Freudian psychoanalysis in its otherwise spiritual approach.

But the immediate predecessor of AA was the Oxford Group Movement/Moral Re-Armament, a Christian evangelical program—complete with regular meetings—designed to help people turn their lives around by finding God and turning their lives and wills over to Him. Both Bill Wilson and Dr. Bob Smith were members of the Oxford Groups when they founded what was to become AA. Lemanski covers this history and does so with great precision. Better yet, he doesn't overwork it but gives us just enough to understand from whence we came.

In addition, he covers the early history of AA, from its origin in 1935 through its heyday in the 1970s and 1980s, to its leveling off in the mid-to-late 1990s, and the beginning of its decline in the present day. He also covers the birth and growth of the disease concept of addiction.

The growth of this concept parallels the growth of AA and in fact is wedded to the 12-Step movement. Lemanski analyzes the reasons for widespread acceptance of the disease model, and also the many inconsistencies in its application.

For instance, if alcoholism and drug addiction is a disease with physical origins, why would we recommend, as treatment, a religious or spiritual program which encourages us to make a connection with God and revamp our moral lives? Lemanski describes this obvious contradiction and shows how addiction treatment in America evolved, in spite of this, into an AA-dominated industry.

He also includes an analysis of AA's efficacy as a treatment program. I believe it is essential for every treatment professional working in the field today to be aware of this information. It would help program managers, therapists, and counselors to realize, first, that AA doesn't work for everybody (indeed it works for a surprisingly small percentage of clients) and, second, that we can help more clients achieve lasting recovery by offering a broad array of treatment modalities and by matching each client to the modalities that work best for him or her.

This latter approach, called client-treatment matching, will soon become the gold standard of addiction treatment. As scientific research proves the efficacy of more and more therapies and treatment modalities in treating addictions, an increasing number of treatment professionals will begin offering these as part of the standard fare.

What are some of these alternative treatments? Lemanski answers this too. He gives snapshot reviews of various treatment modalities and types of therapies, all of which have been proven successful with some significant percentage of clients. He also provides overviews of the nonreligious "alternative" (to AA) self-help organizations.

Today, it's up to each treatment professional to know these alternative treatments and to be prepared to offer them directly to clients or to make referrals so that clients can access these treatments elsewhere. Sadly, very few professionals do this today. But when treatment professionals become more savvy, then the addiction treatment field will compare well with its sister field of psychology. Within the past hundred years, psychology grew from one primary psychotherapeutic intervention, Freudian psychoanalysis, to the dozens upon dozens of often-successful interventions which are used today.

With this book, Lemanski offers not only a remarkably exciting read, but an immensely important work. I feel that everyone associated with the addictions treatment industry can benefit by reading it. As Goethe said, "Those who do not understand the past are doomed to re-live it." We need not re-live the nightmares of addiction treatment past. We can move ahead.

The path is clear.

—Jerry Dorsman

Jerry Dorsman, B.A.C., is the author of two books on addictions, *How to Quit Drinking Without AA* (1991) and *How to Quit Drugs for Good* (1998). He works as an addictions therapist for Upper Bay Counseling and Support Services in Elkton, MD.

Preface

More than a decade ago, Dr. William R. Miller outlined the European multiple-approach model to addictions treatment and predicted that its starkly contrasting methodology would eventually affect the one-size-fits-all U.S. system.[1] In a subsequent article entitled "Beyond Genetic Criteria: Reflections on Life After Clinical Science Wins," Miller and Dr. Robert J. Meyers discussed the efforts of the American Psychological Association (APA) to establish guidelines requiring controlled scientific studies to be the primary source of evidence for therapeutic effectiveness. In a confessional of sorts, the APA has conceded that a large measure of current addictions treatment is based more on religion than science. Currently the APA Task Force on Psychological Intervention Guidelines is promoting long overdue changes via the institution of science-based clinical practice.[2]

Researcher G. Alan Marlatt has listed the reasons for this trend toward reform. Among those he cites, the following are particularly relevant:

• Drinking is a risk behavior, not a disease. The drinking is one thing, the disease consequence is another. [In other words, the *behavior* of drinking can produce disease *consequences*, such as cirrhosis, but drinking in itself is not a disease, just a behavior. As another disease model critic put it, "Smoking is a behavior. Emphysema is a disease."]

• Unlike biological disease, alcoholism can be eliminated or arrested by a voluntary decision by the drinker.

• Unlike with most diseases, many people resolve alcohol problems on their own, without treatment (e.g., maturing out, "spontaneous remission").

• Belief in the disease model of alcoholism predicts greater relapse ... [A recent NIAAA-funded study at the University of New Mexico found that in a traditional 12-step treatment program the greater clients' belief in the disease model, the higher their likelihood of relapsing.][3]

Unfortunately, all of this has amounted to a drop in the metaphorical bucket. *The National Treatment Center Summary Report*, an analysis of 450 addictions treatment programs, estimates that more than 93% of addictions treatment programs are still 12-step programs.[4] These programs are based on the AA-generated disease concept of alcoholism, and are largely variations on the outdated "Minnesota Model" of addictions treatment, which was formulated during the 1950s by the Hazelden Foundation in Minnesota (hence the term, "Minnesota Model"). This model, whose core is Alcoholics Anonymous, has served as the standard in American addictions treatment for decades.

However, clinical studies have shown that this approach to addictions treatment is ineffective. These studies have included a multiple-decades longitudinal study by George Vaillant, et al.,[5] a massive Census Bureau-conducted study,[6] controlled studies of AA's effectiveness,[7][8] and three meta-analyses of virtually all available controlled studies of different treatment modalities and their effectiveness (over 200 studies in all).[9][10][11] These constitute the best scientific evidence regarding addictions treatment efficacy, and their overwhelming conclusion is that AA, 12-step treatment, and its various components are simply not effective means of dealing with addictions—and that several nonreligious addictions treatments are in fact effective, but go virtually unused in the U.S.

That the disease model and 12-step treatment have prevailed has nothing to do with scientific research nor with sound medical principles and practices. Rather, 12-step treatment has prevailed because it was, and still is, the only approach accepted by the American addictions treatment community. The existing system is largely a product of politics and money. The Hughes Act of 1970 channeled billions of tax and insurance dollars into 12-step treatment, and the programs which grew as a result see no reason to change.

Although those who promote AA, 12-step treatment, and the disease concept have promoted alcohol dependence as a "disease," it has *never* been treated as such in the U.S. As we saw above, the best scientific evidence is routinely ignored by the treatment community, which clings to an approach with virtually no scientific evidence of efficacy. As well, normal medical principles (such as the principle of informed consent) are routinely violated by 12-step treatment providers. And 12-step providers do not even pay attention to the extremely shaky "scientific" evidence on which they base their programs. More specifically, they pay no attention to the numerous classifications and subclassifications of alcoholism propounded by the father of the disease concept, E.M. Jellinek, and his followers. Instead, they've produced a type of treatment based on only one subtype—so-called gamma alcoholism.

Initially, following passage of the Hughes Act, the implementation of treatment on a national scale required a broad-brush approach in order to be acceptable to the U.S. Congress. A national program required a streamlined approach with factory-like efficiency, and the 12-steps and a simplified disease model provided that one-size-fits-all approach. It was a simplistic quick fix to an extremely complex problem. That it has worked poorly should surprise no one.

The fundamentally flawed and outdated U.S. addictions treatment model has led to the neglect, misdiagnosis, and improper treatment of addicted and nonaddicted alcohol abusers. As Terence Gorski, a prominent spokesman within the treatment field, writes:

> When people came to us for help, we took two inexcusable positions that said: Take treatment you don't need or keep drinking until you get really sick, then come back. Both of these positions were stock and trade in many chemical dependency programs.[12]

The problem is, in fact, even worse than Gorski indicates, because massive numbers of individuals who are not even alcohol or drug abusers, let alone alcohol or drug dependent, have been coerced into attending 12-step treatment since it was instituted on a national scale. This has gone on because of the unquestioning acceptance by the public (fostered by AA's front groups, hidden members in the media, and by treatment providers) that the 12-step approach is the only one that works, and the concomitant belief that anyone forced into treatment belongs there. This has allowed treatment centers to operate virtually without scrutiny and to charge what the market will bear without having to produce evidence of efficacy. In essence, politics, money, and religious beliefs, rather than sound medical practice, have prevailed.

Change is long overdue. It's time for accountability and consumer protection in the addictions treatment field. Unfortunately, a good majority of the practitioners within the field—people who one would expect to embrace treatment modalities with good scientific evidence of efficacy (and which are, by and large, much less expensive than 12-step treatment) —are resisting such improvements tooth and nail.

Change will not come easily. This is largely a result of pro-12-step bias within the treatment field. A majority of treatment professionals are themselves members of 12-step recovery programs and are very attached to them. They are so attached, in fact, there is a taboo within the field against *any* criticism of 12-step programs, especially criticism which questions the efficacy and supposed necessity of such programs.

This 12-step bias is insidious because it prevents the implementation of a variety of other more effective treatment approaches. It is also insidious because it is in large measure invisible. Beneath the veneer of professional sounding terminology and apparent professionalism lurks a moral imperative: psychic surrender via the 12 steps. This is a very real and central part of both the self-help movement and professional treatment, and one can hardly expect those who have plunged themselves into such religious "surrender" to be objective about it, its effects, or the programs that promote it. For this reason, standard addictions treatment in the U.S. continues to remain largely ineffective, and a majority of treatment providers remain oblivious, in fact hostile, to more effective approaches.

The controversy over which treatments are effective has been raging for decades. Unfortunately, this debate is not academic. The lives and health of millions of chemically dependent people lie in the balance.

In a small way, I hope to make some contribution in this area; I hope that I can help to initiate change. Hence this book.

1. "Haunted by the Zeitgeist," by William M. Miller. *Annals of the New York Academy of Science*, 1986, No. 472, pp. 110–129.
2. "Beyond Generic Criteria: Reflections on Life After Clinical Science Wins," by William R. Miller and Robert J. Meyers. *Clinical Science*, Spring 1995, pp. 2–6.
3. "Alcoholism: Disease or Addiction?," by G. Alan Marlatt and Terence Gorski. *Professional Counselor*, October 1996.
4. *National Treatment Center Study Summary Report*, Paul Roman and Terry Blum, principal investigators. Athens, GA: Institute for Behavioral Research, 1997, p. 13.
5. *The Natural History of Alcoholism Revisited*, by George Vaillant. Cambridge, MA: Harvard University Press, 1995.
6. "Correlates of Past-Year Status Among Treated and Untreated Persons with Former Alcohol Dependence: United States, 1992," by Deborah Dawson. *Alcoholism: Clinical and Experimental Research*, 1996, Vol. 20, pp. 771–779.
7. *Outpatient Treatment of Alcoholism*, by Jeffrey Brandsma, et al. Baltimore: University Park Press, 1980.
8. "A Controlled Experiment on the Use of Court Probation for Drunk Arrests," by Keith Ditman, et al. *American Journal of Psychiatry*, August 1967, pp. 64–67.
9. *Handbook of Alcoholism Treatment Approaches, Second Edition*, Reid Hester and William Miller, eds. Boston: Allyn & Bacon, 1995.
10. "The Cost Effectiveness of Treatment for Alcoholism: A First Approximation," by H.D. Holder, et al. *Journal of Studies on Alcohol*, 1991, Vol. 52, pp. 517–540.
11. "The Cost Effectiveness of Treatment for Alcoholism: A Second Approximation," by John Finney and Rudolf Moos. *Journal of Studies on Alcohol*, 1996, Vol. 57, pp. 229–242.
12. Marlatt and Gorski, op. cit.

1

The Early American Recovery Movement

The first advocate of the disease concept of alcoholism was Doctor Benjamin Rush. Rush was born in Philadelphia in 1745, and at an early age decided to embark upon a career in medicine. He graduated from the College of New Jersey at Princeton and, undertook advanced studies in Europe. In 1769, Rush returned to America and became the first professor of medicine at the University of Pennsylvania. In addition, as a political activist, he was one of the plotters of the American Revolution and was a member of the Continental Congress. His name appears on the Declaration of Independence.

During the Revolution, Rush was Physician-General of the Continental Army and was in charge of troop hospitals. While tending the soldiers and observing their condition and behavior, he concluded that heavy consumption of hard alcohol was more destructive of fighting effectiveness than were the British.

In 1778, Rush published a document called "Directions for Preserving the Health of Soldiers." In this document, he exposed several common myths concerning alcohol consumption. First, he refuted the widespread belief that hard liquor was a tonic and provided health benefits. He targeted notions that alcohol could protect soldiers against heat, cold, fevers, and camp diseases. Second, Rush refuted the notion that alcohol has nutritional value. Finally, he stated that alcohol consumed in large quantities has a pronounced debilitating effect on soldiers.[1]

After the triumph of the American Revolution, Dr. Rush retired from the army and devoted himself to study of the relationship between the mind and the body. His research encompassed the effects of the intemperate use of alcohol. In 1784, he published a 40-page pamphlet called *Inquiry into the Effects of Spiritous Liquors on the Human Body and Mind.* This booklet contained the first comprehensive attack upon the use of hard alcohol. Rush argued that rather than providing medicinal benefits, hard liquor actually aggravated most diseases and was the cause of many others. Rush described alcohol as habit forming, contributing to memory loss, and eventually leading to a progressive moral and physical decay. Rush described an addict's condition: "In folly it causes him to resemble a calf; in stupidity, an ass; in roaring, a mad bull; in quarreling and fighting, a dog; in cruelty, a tiger; in fetor, a skunk; in filthiness, a hog; and in obscenity, a he-goat."[2]

Rush's pamphlet included a chart which was described as a "Moral and Physical Thermometer of Intemperance." The scale starts at zero and climbs to a high of 80, and lists types of alcoholic beverages consumed and their supposed resultant vices, diseases, and punishments. For instance, grog and brandy and water (rated at 30), according to Rush, leads to fighting, horse-racing, inflamed eyes, red nose and face, and black eyes and rags.[3]

Rush also specified the diseases which he believed were caused by excessive consumption of alcohol:

1. Decay of appetite, sickness at stomach, puking of bile and discharging of frothy and viscous phlegm.
2. Obstruction of the liver.
3. Jaundice and dropping of belly and limbs, and finally every cavity of the body.
4. Hoarseness and a husky cough, leading to consumption.
5. Diabetes, i.e., a frequent and weakening discharge of pale or sweetish urine.
6. Redness and eruptions in different parts of the body, rumbuds, a form of leprosy.
7. A fetid breath.
8. Frequent and disgusting belchings.
9. Epilepsy.
10. Gout.
11. Madness—one-third of patients confined owed their condition to ardent spirits. Most of the diseases are of a mortal nature. [4]

Editions of Rush's document were distributed and exhausted as quickly as they were printed. Excerpts were reprinted in newspapers and magazines and were widely read throughout the country. While in some respects Dr. Rush lacked eloquence, the substance of what he had to say possessed great credibility.

Unlike a majority of those members of the temperance movement who would later support and eventually vote for prohibition, Rush did not advocate total abstinence from alcoholic beverages. In *American Temperance Movements*, Jack S. Blocker, Jr. states:

Rush resolved the contradiction between the two views of alcoholic beverages as dangerous and beneficial by assigning alcohol's dangerous qualities to distilled spirits and its beneficial effects to the fermented beverages. . . . He recommended substitutes: water, cider, malt liquors, wines, molasses or vinegar in water, coffee, tea, and, in certain circumstances, opium.[5][6]

Numerous civic and church leaders responded positively to Rush's views. After his death in 1813, his pamphlet continued to be reprinted for decades and continued to be a source of inspiration for the American Temperance Movement.

Growth of the Temperance Movement

In 1808 in New York state, a physician named Billy J. Clark organized America's first temperance society after reading Dr. Rush's publication. Under Dr. Clark's leadership, the Union Temperance Society of Moreau and Northumberland drafted the first temperance constitution which included an abstinence pledge regarding distilled spirits. Initially, this pledge lasted a one-year test period. At the end of this test period, members came forward to provide public testimonials to the benefits of hard-liquor abstinence. As news of these testimonials spread, many other temperance societies quickly began to organize throughout the United States.[7]

Another early temperance leader was the Reverend Lyman Beecher of Litchfield, Connecticut. Also influenced by the Rush document, Beecher preached a series of sermons to his congregation in 1825, which were compiled and published in 1826 as *Six Sermons on the Nature, Occasions, Signs, Evils and Remedy for Intemperance*. Here, Beecher vividly described and condemned the evils of alcohol. In addition to adding an evangelical tone to the temperance movement, Beecher called for "banishment of ardent spirits from the list of lawful articles of commerce."[8] In other words, he advocated prohibition.

In 1829, the nation's first temperance newspaper, *The Philanthropist*, chronicled the growth of temperance societies across America. By mid-1830, such societies blanketed the nation, and the ideas originally proposed by Benjamin Rush were largely forgotten; Rush's vision of a healthy nation enjoying moderate quantities of beer and wine was no longer acceptable. From this time on—until passage of the 18th amendment to the U.S. Constitution—the "temperance" movement advocated complete prohibition of all alcoholic beverages.[9]

The Washingtonian Society

In 1849, six self-described drunkards who habitually engaged in drinking bouts at Chase's Tavern in Baltimore, founded what became the Washingtonian Society. After being moved by a temperance lecture given by the Reverend Matthew Smith of New York, they decided to terminate their nightly drinking and to form an abstinence society named after George Washington. They then took a pledge to abstain from all intoxicating beverages. These men began to conduct and attend regular "experience meetings" in which the theme was simple: fellow drunkards would testify and confess to the misery and sin produced in their lives as the result of alcohol consumption, and then provide joyous testimony regarding the benefits flowing from the pledge to abstain. The rules were basic. Only those afflicted by alcohol abuse were allowed to attend and to tell their stories. The Washingtonian Society was set up to be a self-help organization in which drunkards could help and encourage other drunkards to maintain their abstinence pledge. One component of the Washingtonian program was similar to that of Alcoholics Anonymous: Washingtonians, like AA members, were encouraged to spread the message; specifically, each Washingtonian member was expected to locate another drunkard and bring this individual to meetings. This friend was then expected to do the same so that the organization would grow.

By the early 1840s, temperance was more than ever in the news, and the Washingtonians were receiving increasing publicity. One year after formation of the original group, delegations of Washingtonians were active in other parts of the country, and the first anniversary celebration of the organization in Baltimore produced the largest temperance demonstration to date.

The Society made a genuine attempt to provide its members with elements which previous temperance organizations had failed to supply. For example, Washingtonians helped to provide material assistance in the form of food, clothing, and temporary shelter for those in need. In addition, the society helped drunkards who were in legal trouble post bail and pay fines. These projects were financed by wealthy supporters and by the Martha Washington Society. Women in this adjunct society raised money through a variety of activities, and created alternatives to saloon attendance such as picnics, concerts, and group singing.[10]

Although well intentioned, the Washingtonians failed to endure. The rapid growth initially experienced by the organization was followed by an equally rapid decline. There were several reasons for this. First, the Washingtonians were a loosely knit organization, and the quality of the "experience meetings" varied greatly from community to community. Often a delegation of Washingtonians would converge upon a town with a great deal of attendant publicity and fanfare. After the departure of such delegations, life in the community would usually return to normal; enthusiasm would diminish, and attendance at Washingtonian meetings and related activities would decline. Second, the quantity and quality of social assistance varied widely from place to place. This was aggravated by large influxes of new members, which overwhelmed the finances of the Washingtonians in many communities. The high expectations of many new members were thereby dashed, and they dropped their membership in the group.

In the final analysis, however, the Washingtonians' decline mainly reflected what contemporary addictions research reveals: moral persuasion, in and of itself, is not adequate to successful maintenance of abstinence for the vast majority of individuals wishing to overcome a serious addiction. Many Washingtonian members who had signed "the pledge" were seen shortly afterwards engaging in their former drinking activities. This, in the eyes of many, diminished the credibility of the organization and resulted in diminished physical, moral, and financial support. Although some remnants of the movement would continue, by 1845 Washingtonianism was dead as a social movement.[11]

Fraternal Temperance Societies

Many former Washingtonians who desired to remain active within the temperance movement became involved in fraternal societies. Of these societies, the Sons of Temperance was probably the largest and best known. Founded in New York City in 1842, this organization embraced many of the positive elements in the Washingtonian movement while eliminating many of its flaws. Like the Washingtonians, the Sons of Temperance provided moral and financial support to its members. However, the financial support provided to members and their families was given under a codified system of contributions and benefits. The organization was self-supporting and kept its economic independence through collecting a prescribed amount of fees and dues. As it grew in membership, strict central control was maintained by elected officers. Members were required to sign "the pledge" and to be strictly abstinent from all intoxicating beverages; in addition, membership benefits were available only to members in good standing.

The Sons of Temperance also practiced what would later become known as "anonymity." To quote author Jack S. Blocker, Jr.:

The Washingtonians were occasionally embarrassed by public backsliding on the part of those who signed their pledge. The Sons adopted a policy of secrecy to remove the liability of public exposure from both the organization and its individual members; in doing so they anticipated a basic principle in Alcoholics Anonymous.[12]

In short, the individual backsliding member could effectively be protected from humiliation and public shame through this policy; equally, the organization could be protected from public revelation of its failures.

As with the Washingtonians, the Sons had an adjunct, the Sisters of Temperance. However, this adjunct focused to a much larger extent on women's issues than the Martha Washington Society. Organizationally similar to its male counterpart, the Sisters established the first temperance newspaper completely managed by women. The *New York Olive Plant* was founded in 1842 and provided a woman-centered view of temperance activities. In addition, the organization established a house of employment (that is, an employment agency) to assist abstinent women in the attainment of decent employment with fair compensation.[13]

The Civil War delivered a blow to temperance activities within the United States. Issues of North versus South superseded issues of wet versus dry. In addition, in 1862 the federal government imposed a tax on every retail liquor establishment and manufacturer. This taxation was not a trivial matter; during the years 1870 to 1915 this liquor tax generated between one-half and two-thirds of the tax revenue generated by the federal government.[14]

Women's Growing Involvement in Temperance Societies

The end of the Civil War produced a revival in temperance activities. Fraternal societies which had lost membership during the war again began to increase in size, and women began taking a more active role within the movement. This was best expressed within the Women's Christian Temperance Union. Oddly enough, this women's movement was initially inspired by a man.

Dr. Dioclesian Lewis was a preacher, social reformer, feminist, health, and temperance movement activist. He was said to have walked into saloons leading an entourage of loyal followers to pray for the souls of those within. During lectures given in churches, he praised these "visitation bands" as powerful tools for reform. In 1873, his message reached and inspired Elizabeth Thompson of Hillsboro, Ohio. Although 60 years old at the time, Mrs. Thompson took up the crusade. After an emotionally charged meeting in a local church, "Mother Thompson," as she came to be called, proceeded with her group of mostly female activists to the most conspicuous liquor dealer in Hillsboro. William Smith, the store owner, watched from inside as the marchers picketed and prayed outside his store. The women were adamant and emotionally charged. In the end, Smith publicly pledged to stop selling liquor. Mother Thompson viewed this victory as a sign of things to come and led her followers on to greater victories. The crusade gained public notice and strength, finally leading to the creation of the Women's Christian Temperance Union (WCTU) in 1874. Women activists from 17 states, inspired by Mother Thompson, convened in Cleveland, Ohio and elected Frances Elizabeth Willard as their first president. Willard, a strong activist and a well educated former university professor, soon organized chapters in virtually every state.[15]

The WCTU eventually managed to win legislation which required instruction to students in all public schools on the harmful effects of alcohol consumption. Ultimately it became a formidable lobby which would tip the balance toward making prohibition possible in America.

The WCTU was in reality the first mass women's movement in America. During the 19th century, women were treated more as property than as citizens. The Union effectively gave women more power, control, and a voice within the existing social system. The battle against alcohol and intemperance precipitated a fundamental change in American attitudes and an increased demand by women for equal rights. An anonymous letter published by the *New York Herald Tribune* in 1859 puts the matter well:

> To deny her the use of that most efficient weapon, a vote, and then urge her into a contest with the liquor trade is like saying that women cannot use artillery . . . but ought to form the advance in an attack on an army of men well drilled in their use, sending them forward with broadswords, javelins, and other implements of medieval warfare.[16]

Temperance/Prohibition as a Political Movement

Until 1869, most of the efforts toward reform had taken place on the local and state levels. In that year, 500 delegates convened in Chicago to draft a platform and to organize a national political party, the Prohibition Party. National prohibition of alcoholic beverages was its core issue, and in itself it was never enough to turn the Prohibition Party into a ruling party. The Prohibitionists did, however, command strength through providing swing votes on a number of other socio-political issues. They also succeeded in keeping prohibition in the spotlight as a national political issue, and they kept other social issues, such as a woman's right to vote, in the limelight.

Although the new party's first attempt at introducing a national prohibition amendment failed in 1876, that effort produced a great deal of publicity. This shifted the focus of the temperance movement. The Washingtonians and fraternal societies were primarily nonpolitical and self-help oriented; the later temperance activists realized that imposition of social reform required legislative action and political strength. Temperance thus became a national political issue.

Frances Willard and the WCTU endorsed the Prohibition Party in 1884. Willard and a majority of the members of the WCTU believed that the old and established political parties would not fully support the prohibition cause. This endorsement caused a split within the WCTU and a walkout by several of its members. One of these disaffected members, J. Ellen Foster of Iowa, along with several other former WCTU members, founded the Non-Partisan Women's Christian Temperance Union. This did little to slow down the WCTU, which remained very much political and continued to grow, doubling its membership during the 1880s.[17]

The Anti-Saloon League was the next organization to arise within the framework of the larger temperance movement. Founded by Howard Russell, a Protestant clergyman from Ohio, the group established itself on a national scale in 1896. The League had as its ultimate goal the closing down of all drinking establishments within the United States. This organization ultimately became one of the most successful political machines in the nation.

In 1903, the Anti-Saloon League changed leadership. Reverend Purley A. Baker of Ohio became its new national superintendent. Baker was a cold political realist who played all of the political parties off against one another to further the interests of the League. His group raised and spent large sums of money on lobbying efforts and propaganda literature. In addition to having full-time paid organizers, the League could mobilize thousands of volunteer speakers to further the cause. These political/ organizational efforts produced results. Many aspirants to political office were well aware of the League's power and knew that a lack of League backing could well lead to political defeat.[18]

While those who supported the temperance movement viewed prohibition as the cure-all for solving the problem of alcohol abuse and its related miseries in America, many within the American medical and scientific communities were not naive enough to believe that banning the legal sale of alcohol would solve this problem. Others shared this more pragmatic view. These included those who had to deal with alcohol abuse and related problems on a daily basis, such as law enforcement and penal personnel.

Early Medical/Scientific Treatment of Drinking Disorders

The first voices to suggest that drinking-related problems might best be treated in a medical setting were Dr. Samuel Woodward, the first super-intendent of the Worcester State Hospital in Massachusetts, and Dr. Eli Todd of the Connecticut Medical Society in Hartford, Connecticut. In the 1830s, both men suggested the creation of special institutions for the housing and treatment of inebriates, and the creation of an organization to study the illness concept of inebriety.

The first attempt, of sorts, at creating such a treatment institution was a group home opened for inebriates in Boston in 1841. This home was sponsored by the Washingtonian Society and was eventually forced to close because its funding vanished along with that Society. It was, however, reopened in 1857 when it received other funding. Fairly shortly thereafter, other institutions came into existence for the purpose of treating drunkards. In 1868, the New York State Inebriate Asylum was opened in Binghamton under the direction of Dr. Joseph E. Turner. In 1869, the New York City Asylum was opened for the same purpose, and was operated by the Board of Charities of New York City in conjunction with the New York City Police Department. In addition, at least 11 other nonprofit hospitals and homes for inebriates had come into existence by 1874.

In 1872, the individuals managing these institutions formed a society for the study of inebriety which ultimately became known as the Medical Association for the Study of Inebriety and Narcotics. In 1876, this association began publication of *The Journal of Inebriety*, which described itself as devoted to the study of "spirit and drug neurosis." This periodical remained in operation for 38 years. During its lifetime it published approximately 700 papers of which roughly 100 were devoted either entirely or partially to the idea that inebriety was an illness, the most prominent themes being that inebriety was a neurosis or a psychosis, that alcohol was a precipitating cause, and that its consumption was a symptom of a pre-existing psychological condition.

The Association and its publication lasted until 1914, a few years prior to the passage of the 18th Amendment. The views of this organization and its periodical were not widely accepted by the American medical establish-ment. A majority of practicing physicians adhered to the temperance-prohibition mentality that viewed the problem of alcohol abuse as a moral problem rather than as a medical illness.

Only after the repeal of prohibition did the medical establishment begin to seriously consider the disease concept of inebriety. And only after prohibition ended was the malady commonly referred to as "alcoholism."[19]

The Religious Nature of the Temperance Movement

The religious nature of the temperance movement can best be exemplified by one of its most famous crusaders, Carry Amelia Nation. Born in Kentucky in 1846, Nation was in her fifties when she became inspired by and committed herself to the temperance crusade. While living with her husband in Medicine Lodge, Kansas, she had personal conversations with God and visions of mortal, hand-to-hand combat with Satan. She believed it an omen that her father had misspelled her name as "Carry" rather than "Carrie," and that her name meant that she was destined to fight with God against Satan and "carry a nation" in the movement for temperance. As president of the county WCTU, she conducted her crusade. With hatchet in hand, she carried out numerous saloon-smashing raids; these raids inspired others and kept Nation in newspaper headlines for more than a decade. She died in 1911 and never lived to witness the enactment of the 18th Amendment or its consequences and eventual repeal.[20]

The evangelical nature of the crusade was also exemplified by William Jennings Bryan, three-time Democratic presidential nominee, former Secretary of State, paid lobbyist for the Anti-Saloon League, and staunch supporter of prohibition. Bryan stated:

> We must turn our energies to other countries until the whole world is brought to understand that alcohol is man's greatest enemy. Thus it is a fortunate thing that the abdication of the Kaiser and the fall of arbitrary power came the same year as does the fall of the brewery autocracy and that those two evils came down together. . . . Now we can go for the evangelization of the world on the subject of intoxicating liquor.[21]

This message was repeated after the Allied victory in the First World War by Ernest Cherrington, Anti-Saloon League president. During the peace conference in France, he stated:

> Our imperative demands are not limited to the [Versailles] Peace Conference. The important need for temperance reform must be recognized in the reconstruction program of several nations of Europe. . . . The time has come for the formation of an international league for the extermination of [alcoholic] beverage traffic throughout the world.[22]

This heady rhetoric more than hints at the fact that many temperance zealots genuinely believed that prohibition was fated to be the ultimate salvation of mankind.

The Coming of Prohibition

After the Allies scored a resounding victory in the "war to end all wars," a great many Americans were demanding reform in regard to alcohol. A demand for some kind of prohibition had been voiced in this country for more than a century, and a majority of voting Americans wanted to get on with it.

The answer to their desires came from Andrew J. Volstead, an ultra-religious Republican congressman from Minnesota. Volstead drafted a proposed 18th Amendment to the U.S. Constitution banning the import, transport, sale, and export of "intoxicating liquors." This Amendment passed Congress in May 1917 and was ratified by the states in very short order; Nebraska ratified the Amendment in January 1919 and it became, for the time being, a part of the Constitution. The Amendment, however, required enabling legislation, which Volstead supplied; the Volstead Act passed Congress in October 1919. It prescribed a one-year grace period prior to implementation (dated from the time of ratification of the 18th Amendment by the states), so on January 20, 1920 national prohibition became a reality in the United States.

The Volstead Act did provide certain exemptions in regard to the sale of alcohol: grain natural spirits in the form of industrial alcohol was exempt, as were sacramental wine, patent medicines, doctor's prescriptions, toiletries, food flavoring extracts, syrups, vinegar, cider, and malt beverages with no more than .5% alcohol content ("near beer"). During the next decade many Americans would find clever ways to take advantage of these exemptions in order to legally circumvent the law. Others would seize the opportunity to profit by openly violating the law.

What a majority in the temperance movement had not anticipated was the extent to which a relatively large percentage of the American population would be willing to take risk in order to obtain what had legally become forbidden fruit. The Puritan virtues which had inspired the temperance crusade included obedience to God, conformity of thought, and respect for the law. What had been inconceivable to the Puritans and temperance crusaders was that this moral conformity was impossible to achieve, and more impossible still, to enforce through legislation and law enforcement. Moral reformers were convinced that the overwhelming majority of law-abiding Americans would conform to, respect, and obey the provisions of the Volstead Act, even if they initially resented it. They anticipated that their resistance would subside as this once-resentful minority came to enjoy the health, happiness, prosperity and other social benefits that prohibition and its moral imperatives promised. This had been a prominent and recurring theme within temperance organizations from the very beginning. What the former crusaders soon discovered was that many Americans had no desire to follow their coercive, Puritan path, and the 1920s would prove to be one of the most lawless, corrupt, and violent decades in U.S. history.

The Effects of Prohibition

After the imposition of prohibition, the first person to express public concern was former President William Howard Taft. His words were a harbinger of things to come:

> Those who thought that an era of clear thinking and clean living was at hand were living in a fool's paradise. The law had passed . . . against the views and practices of a majority of people in many large cities. . . . The business of manufacturing alcohol, liquor and beer will go out of the hands of law-abiding members of the community and will be transferred to the quasi-criminal classes.[23]

However, to a large extent the exemptions within the Volstead Act made it ridiculously easy to circumvent the law. George de Latour, who owned a vineyard in Napa Valley, made arrangements with the Catholic archbishop of San Francisco to sell sacramental wine to the church. The quantities of wine were so large that it was obvious that priests were reselling the beverage to their parishioners. Yet, since the Volstead Act placed no restrictions on the quantity of wine that the churches could legally purchase, their buying of large quantities of wine was perfectly legal (though their reselling of it was not). Other vineyards made similar arrangements with the Jewish community. According to the National Prohibition Bureau's own estimates, 678 million gallons of such wine were produced between the years 1925 and 1929. Rather than decline, grape production in Napa Valley vineyards increased ten fold between 1920 and 1933.[24]

Beringer Vineyard in the Napa Valley also prospered during prohibition because of loopholes in the Volstead Act. During prohibition, the vineyard marketed raisin cakes or bricks of dried, processed raisins. The Vineyard's marketing strategy was extremely effective. Each raisin cake contained all of the ingredients needed to make wine. Each cake sold also contained a warning label, cautioning the purchaser not to place the contents into a bottle, not to place water into the bottle, not to cork the bottle, and not to allow the contents to ferment for 21 days, because this fermentation would create wine. The warning label was legal, and in essence provided the buyer with the instructions necessary to produce homemade wine.[25]

During prohibition, numerous books and instructional manuals also appeared describing how to make homemade beer and wine, the ingredients for which were all perfectly legal to possess. Soon, the making of such beverages became a popular American hobby.

As well, hard liquor could still be legally purchased at a pharmacy with a doctor's prescription, although the amounts were limited. And patent medicines, many of which contained a large percentage of ethyl alcohol, were also perfectly legal under the Volstead Act.

On the more sinister side, nightclubs, called speakeasies, began to appear all over America. These establishments sold their customers hard liquor, and during prohibition it became fashionable for middle-class Americans to patronize these places. In addition, while the saloon had been a male domain, speakeasies catered to both sexes.

In order for such establishments to exist, a reliable supply of liquor was needed. This liquor had to come from somewhere, and large amounts of it were smuggled across the border. However, most of it did not reach the final consumer without being altered. One good case of Canadian whiskey, for example, could easily be turned into five cases of bootleg whiskey. Mixing it with raw alcohol and water and rebottling it with a counterfeit label increased profits dramatically. So, a majority of illegal stills in this country did not produce whiskey, which required more sophisticated and expensive equipment, but raw alcohol, which was less difficult and less expensive to process. During the first five years of prohibition, federal agents seized 697,000 stills.[26]

Another source of alcohol which could be used to make counterfeit whiskey and gin came from the nation's industrial chemical industry. The Volstead Act contained provisions for the legitimate manufacture of alcohol for industrial applications. A permit was necessary for the purchase of this alcohol, and thousands of chemical companies which existed only on paper appeared and were issued purchasing permits.

Still another source of liquor was the same American distilleries that had been producing it prior to prohibition. These manufacturers could still legally export in bulk unlimited quantities of liquor for "medical purposes." Companies which existed only on paper purchased liquor for shipment abroad, but most of these "shipments" didn't occur; the liquor remained and was consumed in the United States.

Roy A. Haynes, America's first Prohibition Commissioner, commented on one such "shipment" to Scotland. He wrote:

If we believed the tales of all who apply for liquor permits, we would naturally come to the absurd conclusion that the whole world is sick and desperately in need of distilled spirits. . . . Does anyone believe that Scotland, home of whiskey, is really in need of 66,000 gallons of American whiskey for non-beverage purposes? . . . It is the irony of ironies, a wet world come to dry America to beg for liquor.[27]

In reality, just the opposite was happening; rum-running had become widespread and the U.S. Coast Guard found itself overburdened by the impossible task of enforcing the law.

Whatever the source, raw alcohol and some form of smuggled liquor were shipped to what were known as "cutting plants," where they were mixed with water and some type of flavoring, and bottled as whiskey, scotch, vodka, or gin. Counterfeit labels were printed and applied to the bottles, which were packaged to resemble the genuine article. These fakes were then sold to speakeasies or other providers of illegal liquor, and then resold to their respective customers.

This production process produced alcoholic beverages that lacked palatability to the patrons of speakeasies, and so produced a change in American drinking habits. The cocktail, which became fashionable during the 1920s, was invented as a means of diluting bootleg liquor and hiding its horrible taste.[28]

While some of the more famous bootleggers such as George Remus and William McCoy refused to deal in adulterated liquor, they were the exception rather than the rule. (Legend has it that the expression "the real McCoy" was coined in reference to the high quality of the liquor that McCoy sold.) The distribution and illegal sale of alcoholic beverages had fallen into the hands of organized criminal elements who had little concern for standards of chemical purity. In addition to the adulterating chemicals that many bootleggers deliberately introduced into their liquor, poorly manufactured stills often contained fittings which contaminated the alcohol with residual quantities of highly toxic lead.

The result of the consumption of these contaminated beverages was tragic. In 1930, the Prohibition Bureau reported that more than 15,000 victims in one county of Kansas alone required treatment because of harm from some form of contaminated alcohol. Nationally, between 1920 and 1927 more than 50,000 deaths occurred due to consumption of contaminated liquor. This number does not include the many thousands of non-fatal poisonings which resulted in paralysis or blindness.[29]

After eight years in office, Mable Willebrandt, Deputy Attorney General in charge of Prohibition, resigned her post. In the year she did so, 1928, she published a book entitled, *The Inside of Prohibition*. This book documented the political corruption which had become widespread during the prohibition years: "The influence of liquor in politics begins down in the city wards and often in county districts, but it extends if it can up to the

Cabinet and the White House in Washington."[30] The White House reference was to George Remus, who was purported to have sold $75 million worth of liquor in a two-year period, and was said to have spent $20 million to pay off a variety of local, state, and federal officials. Remus made millions of dollars on which he paid no taxes, and he was (at least for the first few years) able to buy or influence his way out of a prison term. Willebrandt further wrote:

> After George Remus, king of the bootleggers, had been convicted and lost his appeals, the rumor reached me that he would never serve a day in Atlanta prison. I set it down as only the bragging of the defendant. But a few days later, a phone call came from the White House, stating that a respite of 60 days would be granted Remus if the Attorney General would send over the necessary papers. Prominent politicians . . . had intervened with the President [Coolidge].[31]

During the 1920s, the violent activities of organized crime became widespread and highly publicized; the names of Al Capone, Dutch Schultz, and a host of other bootleggers and criminals regularly appeared in newspaper headlines. However, as Americans were soon to learn, these news sensations exposed only the tip of a huge, corrupt sociopolitical iceberg.

After his victory in 1928, one of Herbert Hoover's first acts as president was to appoint a 10-man panel to document the results of prohibition. The National Commission on Law Observance and Enforcement was headed by former Attorney General George W. Wickersham. The Wickersham Commission obtained evidence, collected testimony, and conducted a study of the manner in which the provisions of the Volstead Act were being enforced.

The Commission's report was published as a five-volume set in 1931. The report made no major recommendations, suggested no major legislative changes, and offered no clear-cut solutions to the problems it documented. When excerpts reached the press, factions on both the wet and dry sides of the prohibition issue were disappointed. However, one thing was becoming increasingly clear to the American public: the Volstead Act could never be effectively enforced. Tax expenditures for law enforcement had increased dramatically to cover the costs of prosecuting the huge number of alcohol-related cases that clogged the system. Meanwhile, alcohol consumption had actually increased since 1920.[32] Prohibition was eroding American respect for the law on a grand scale; it had made corruption on a grand scale widespread.

Prohibition was not, however, the major focus of the Hoover administration. The stock market crash of 1929 and the plight of the economy dominated its political focus. American humorist Will Rogers voiced the sentiments of the public in 1931 when he was asked to give his views on prohibition. Rogers responded: "What does prohibition amount to, if your neighbors' children are not eating? . . . [F]ood, not drink, is our problem now. We were so afraid the poor people might drink—now we fixed it so they can't eat."[33]

The End of Prohibition

Americans again wanted reform. However, the sociopolitical climate had changed radically during the 1920s. Millions of citizens were now out of work, and very few of them were concerned with the moral imperatives associated with prohibition. As the Great Depression deepened, there was an increasing demand for repeal of the 18th Amendment, not out of moral concerns, but out of pragmatic economic interests.

When Franklin D. Roosevelt defeated Herbert Hoover in the 1932 election, he immediately took steps to initiate repeal. When Roosevelt took office on March 4, 1933, he issued an executive order which effectively reduced appropriations for the Prohibition Bureau by one-half and cut $2 million from the appropriations of the Bureau of Industrial Alcohol. In addition, he submitted to Congress a bill to legalize the sale of beer prior to the full repeal of prohibition, which passed and became effective on April 7, 1933. This legislation imposed a $5-a-barrel tax on beer and required a $1000 license fee. Again, this swift legislation was not the result of high moral concern, but rather represented pure pragmatism. Roosevelt needed to reduce unnecessary government expenditures and to generate new tax revenues to meet the costs of emergency programs to ameliorate the effects of the depression.[34] A 21st Amendment (to end prohibition) was quickly passed by Congress and was submitted to the states for ratification; it passed on December 5, 1933.

The After-Effects of Prohibition

After the end of prohibition, the nation inherited a large and wealthy organized crime underworld, which quickly moved into other criminal activities. This is the largest and most unfortunate legacy of the "Noble Experiment" of prohibition. There were others.

The former temperance reform workers, many of whom had dedicated their lives to prohibition, were thoroughly discredited. Temperance had promised utopian benefits that included health, religious-spiritual enlightenment, prosperity, and the attainment of other lofty ideals. What the Noble Experiment had in fact produced was death, violence, and unprecedented corruption. To say that prohibition was a failure is an understatement. In addition to the above-listed ills, prohibition produced a medical-therapeutic void as regards treatment of addictions.

Prohibition's failure to provide an effective answer to or cure for alcohol abuse or intemperance was another of its major failings. The very people to whom the American temperance movement promised the most were the very people who not only received the least, but suffered the most in the vacuum created in the wake of prohibition's departure. The temperance movement viewed alcohol as a moral problem, and effectively imposed this view upon the public. Those who viewed it as a medical or psychological problem were, for the time being, disenfranchised.

The work of Dr. Benjamin Rush was forgotten. The Washingtonian Society and the fraternal societies that had followed it were gone. The Medical Association for the Study of inebriety and Narcotics, and its *Journal of Inebriety*, were gone. And the other institutions associated with the 19th-century medical and self-help organizations were long since gone. As a result of the temperance movement, medical/scientific research into the causes and effective treatment of addictions had come to a virtual standstill, and effective programs for alcohol- and drug-related problems were almost nonexistent. (It's important to note that both Bill Wilson and Dr. Bob Smith, the co-founders of Alcoholics Anonymous, easily obtained alcohol and suffered full-blown alcohol dependence throughout the prohibition period.)

The temperance movement had placed all of its religious/spiritual eggs in one basket, and that basket had fallen to pieces. In the utopian visions of the temperance mind, medical or psychological treatment for alcoholism/ inebriety was not necessary; people with such problems were not supposed to exist, and if they did, it was because of their moral failings.

So it was in 1935, in this therapeutic near vacuum, that AA co-founder Bill Wilson presented what he considered an effective program for the treatment of alcoholism. Thus it was ultimately a patient with no medical, scientific, psychological, or psychiatric training who provided the basis for the predominant (at least in the United States) form of "modern" alcoholism treatment.

---

1. *The End of the Roaring Twenties: Prohibition and Repeal*, by William Severn. New York: Simon and Schuster, 1969, p. 25.
2. Ibid., pp. 26–27.
3. *Prohibition: Thirteen Years that Changed America*, by Edward Behr. New York: Arcade Publishing, 1996, pp. 15–16.
4. Ibid., p. 16.

5. *American Temperance Movements: Cycles of Reform*, by Jack S. Blocker, Jr. Boston: K.G. Hall & Co., 1989, p. 9.
6. Ibid..
7. Severn, op. cit., pp. 29–30.
8. Ibid., p. 9.
9. Behr, op. cit., p. 11.
10. Blocker, op. cit., pp. 44–45.
11. Ibid., pp. 44–49.
12. Ibid., p. 48.
13. Ibid., p. 49.
14. Severn, op. cit., pp. 48–49.
15. Behr, op. cit., pp. 35–44.
16. Ibid., p. 47.
17. Blocker, op. cit., p. 85.
18. Severn, op. cit., pp. 85–99.
19. *The Disease Concept of Alcoholism*, by E.M. Jellinek. New Haven, CT: Hillhouse Press, 1960, pp. 1–7.
20. Severn, op. cit., pp. 77–79.
21. Behr, op. cit., pp. 73–74.
22. Ibid., p. 77
23. Ibid., p. 78
24. *Prohibition and the Progressive Movement, 1900–1920*, by James Timberlake. Boston, MA: Harvard University Press, 1963, pp. 181–183.
25. Behr, op. cit., p. 80.
26. Ibid., p. 86.
27. Ibid., p. 87.
28. Severn, op. cit., p. 109.
29. Behr, op. cit., p. 133.
30. Ibid., p. 89.
31. Ibid., p. 163.
32. Ibid.
33. Blocker, op. cit., pp. 125–126.
34. Severn, op. cit., p. 167.
35. Ibid., p. 178.

2

Immediate Predecessors of AA

When AA came into being as part of the Oxford Group Movement in the mid and late 1930s, there was a near, but not total, vacuum in the field of alcoholism treatment. The most notable approaches at the time were those of the Salvation Army and the Emmanuel Movement.

The Salvation Army

The most widespread organization dealing with alcoholics, which must have been known to both Bill Wilson and Dr. Bob Smith, was the Salvation Army. This quasi-military group was founded in England by William Booth, who agonized over the plight of England's drunkards and the squalor in which many of them lived. His primary concern was with those individuals who were at the very bottom of the socioeconomic ladder. Booth applied the values of evangelism and fundamentalist religion to the problems and social needs of these individuals.

In America, the Salvation Army employed a variety of tactics in its dealings with alcoholics. In its early days, "Drunkards' Rescue Brigades" were formed which literally went out into the streets to help alcoholics. Subsequently, "inebriate homes" were established to provide shelter, sanitation, housing, and religious instruction for these people. Two Salvation Army "inebriates colonies" were established, one on a Swedish island and the other on an island near New Zealand, which effectively isolated alcoholics from alcohol. Prior to World War I, the organization designated one day a week as "Boozers Day," rounding up as many skid row alcoholics as possible in order to expose them to a gospel meeting. In 1914, individuals who had been converted to God at these meetings banded into a fraternal organization known as the "United Order of Ex-Boozers." This group dedicated itself to rescuing other alcoholics.[1]

Eventually, the Salvation Army applied the rescue mission approach to alcoholism. This approach was based on fundamentalist religion. The healing power of God was mediated through a "conversion experience" (real or feigned) and benevolent, quasi-military authoritarianism. Homeless alcoholics were provided with a place to bathe, a meal, and a safe place to sleep. In exchange for the meal and lodging, prospective converts were exposed to aggressive evangelistic sermons during gospel meetings.

William Booth regarded alcoholism as a disease. He wrote: "After a time the longing for drink becomes a mania. Life seems [as] unsupportable without alcohol as without food. It is a disease often inherited, always developed by indulgence, but as clearly a disease as ophthalmia or stone." Although the Salvation Army has always regarded alcoholism as involving sin, Booth viewed the problem as "a natural outgrowth of our social conditions." "Society," he pointed out, "greases the slope down which these poor creatures slide to perdition."[2]

The rescue mission approach to alcoholism primarily consisted of dependence upon God, a conversion experience leading to acceptance of religious belief, and physical dependence upon the mission. Author Howard J. Cinebell, Jr. describes the problems inherent within the mission approach:

The fact that evangelistic aggressiveness is in some cases a product of disguised hostility is undoubtedly conveyed to the recent or prospective convert, to the detriment of permanent sobriety. Bowery resentment against mission evangelists is in part due to the feeling that they view men and are interested in them only as opportunities to save more souls.

It would be a safe assumption that a high percentage of converts are never assimilated into normal social living. Some of these remain "institutional-ized," living at the mission and doing its work. They have capitulated to the dependent relationship. The fundamental tenet of benevolent authoritarian-ism—"Do what I say and I'll take care of you"—tends to make weaning from immature dependency difficult. Others slip back into the maelstrom of Skid Row. If the individual succeeds in leaving the Bowery and making the difficult break from homelessness, the mission has no structure for con-tinuing the group support which he will continue to need.[3]

During the 1940s and 1950s, the Salvation Army abandoned the mission approach and began what it called the Bowery Corps approach to dealing with alcoholics. The use of food and shelter as "bait" to the homeless alcoholic gave way to a more humane approach. Although the clientele, philosophy, and dynamics remained remarkably similar, in that the program of physical aid and recovery stayed the same, the program now included men's social service centers, which provided work opportunities in the form of industrial homes for destitute men. Likewise, social service departments were incorporated into the organization at this time to work with the families of alcoholics, providing psychiatric counseling and/or other assistance in reconciling the alcoholic with his family. While the new approach continued to embrace "conversion therapy" in rehabilitation, the Salvation Army now incorporated a systematic series of steps for addicts to follow in the conversion process. These read as follows:

1. The alcoholic must realize that he is unable to control his addiction and that his life is completely disorganized.
2. He must realize that only God, his creator, can recreate him as a decent man.
3. He must let God through Jesus Christ rule his life and resolve to live according to His will.
4. He must realize that alcohol addiction is only a symptom of basic defects in his thinking and living, and that the proper use of every talent he possesses is impaired by his enslavement.
5. He should make public confession to God and a man of past wrongdoing and be willing to ask God for guidance in the future.
6. He should make restitution to all whom he has willfully and knowingly wronged.
7. He should realize that he is human and subject to error, and that no advance is made by covering up a mistake; he should admit failure and profit by experience.
8. Since, through prayer and forgiveness, he has found God, he must continue prayerful contact with God and seek constantly to know His will.
9. Because the Salvation Army believes that the personal touch and example are the most vital forces in applying the principles of Christianity, he should be made to work continuously not for his own salvation but to help effect the salvation of others like himself.[4]

One feature of the Bowery Corps program which continued through the 1940s and 1950s was Alcoholic Night. The Salvation Army recognized the special problems associated with alcoholism and set aside one evening per week to address these issues. This evening included a special "street meeting" in front of Salvation Army headquarters to introduce newcomers to the program, and to induce them to attend by way of a brief overview of its benefits and activities.

It was during this period that speakers from Alcoholics Anonymous were first invited to speak to Salvation Army meetings. However, they were eventually barred from Alcoholic Nights. One Bowery Corps officer explained the reason for this restriction: "Some of the A.A. speakers would swear from our platform and say things not in line with our teaching. . . . Most of our institutions have A.A. groups. Here you're either saved or you're not."[5] Many corps officers also apparently objected to the rehashing of old addictions stories, which so often takes place within AA.

Another organization, though, called Alcoholics Victorious, maintained chapters within the Salvation Army. Alcoholics Victorious was founded by the Christian Industrial League of Chicago and, although similar to AA in many respects, it had (and still has) a more fundamentalist Christian orientation and language.[6] Alcoholics Victorious allowed only alcoholic members to attend its weekly meetings in which men provided testimonials, discussed personal issues, and maintained a self-help fellowship.

AA and Skid Row Alcoholics

Alcoholics Anonymous has largely left the problem of skid row alcoholics to specifically Christian groups such as the Salvation Army and Alcoholics Victorious. Author Jacqueline P. Wiseman points out the reasons for this:

> AA has never had much appeal for the lower-class alcoholic. It is primarily a middle-class organization, [which] focuses on helping ex-alcoholics regain their lost status. Skid Row alcoholics dislike what they refer to as "drunkalogs" . . . They dislike what they call the "snottiness" and the "holier-than-thou" attitude of the reformed alcoholic . . . The only reason Skid Row men go to AA is to convince another person . . . that they are trying to lick the alcohol problem.[7]

The Emmanuel Movement

In addition to the Salvation Army and similar evangelical Christian organizations, the Emmanuel Movement was active at the time that Alcoholics Anonymous was in its formative years. This movement was founded in 1906 by Elwood Worcester of Boston. Worcester, an Episcopal clergyman, held a Ph.D. from Leipzig University, where he studied under Wilhelm Wundt, founder of the first psychological laboratory, and physicist-psychologist Gustav Fechner. Worcester believed that the church and physicians should work together in dealing with alcoholism.

The Emmanuel program consisted of three components: 1) group therapy administered through classes; 2) individual therapy administered by Episcopal priests and clinic staff; and 3) a system of social work and individual attention provided by volunteer workers. The program was conducted by individual parishes, and the movement grew rapidly. By 1909, it had spread to England where it was called the Church and Medical Union. Its early years, both in Britain and the U.S., witnessed rapid growth and expansion, though it was constrained by financial/resource limitations. During one six-month period, the Emmanuel Clinic in Boston received more than 5,000 applications by mail, and of these only 125 could be accepted.

In 1929, Worcester resigned from the Boston parish and the movement became incorporated as the Craigie Foundation. It blended religion and psychotherapy in the treatment of alcoholism. Group therapy was offered through weekly meetings. A typical meeting began in church with the singing of familiar hymns, after which a Bible lesson was read, then the Apostle's Creed, and after that requests for prayers in special cases. After the religious portion of the meeting ended, a speaker who was an expert in psychology or neurology would address the group on topics that included habit, anger, suggestion, insomnia, nervousness, what the will could do, and what prayer could do. In this manner, alcoholics were lumped together with those suffering from other maladies who were also treated at the church clinic.

Individual therapy was administered by priests and lay staff. It is noteworthy that this organization developed and utilized the concept of the lay therapist, a nonmedical paraprofessional who specializes in the treatment of alcoholics. This blend of religion and therapy is not at all dissimilar to the Minnesota Model of alcoholism treatment, which was formulated in the 1940s and 1950s and which blends AA and therapy in the treatment of alcoholism.

In terms of individual treatment, the center of Emmanuel therapy was the clinic. Prior to admission, a patient was required to have a physical examination, and in some cases an examination, by a psychiatrist. This was in essence a screening process in which individuals with psychosis or biological pathology were identified and refused admission. After patients were diagnosed as treatable, their applications were accepted and they were directed to the rector's study for psychotherapy. In the treatment of individual alcoholics, Worcester believed that each patient should be seen every day while in the early stages of treatment. The adoption of non-alcoholic habits was suggested to clients during psychotherapy, and supported by the therapist on a daily basis until such habits emerged. The entire process took several months, after which the patient would meet with the therapist once or twice a week. The therapy also included "full self-evaluation." This self-evaluation served to produce catharsis and "unlock the hidden wholesomeness" of the patient's inner life. Worcester also used hypnosis in order to increase patients' suggestibility. Over the history of the movement, Worcester embraced the works of Sigmund Freud and gradually incorporated the use of psychoanalytic techniques into therapy sessions.[8]

Worcester encountered the problem of breaking the addictive cycle long enough for therapy to take effect. His solution consisted of two parts: first, making the analysis brief; and second, combining psychoanalysis with therapeutic suggestion and hypnosis. Unlike what took place within the former temperance organizations, forgiveness was not achieved by turning one's life and will over to an authoritarian God, but rather by modifying the superego of the client; and rather than focus on sin, the Emmanuel approach addressed the underlying cause of harmful behaviors, the sick personality.

This approach also recognized the alcoholic's need for individual and group support during recovery. The "friendly visitor" program provided a buddy system of individual sponsorship, church-related activities, and the assistance of a social services case worker. Through this program, trained social workers helped the alcoholic find employment, helped with finances, and helped with the readjustments necessary to rebuilding family life.

The Emmanuel Movement was the first organized attempt to integrate religion, sociology, psychotherapy, and medicine in the treatment of alcoholism. Through insight gained in treating alcoholics, Worcester arrived at the following understanding of alcoholism:

> The analysis, as a rule, brings to light certain experiences, conflicts, a sense of inferiority, maladjustment to life, and psychic tension, which are the predisposing causes of excessive drinking. Without these, few men become habitual drunkards. In reality drunkenness is a result of failure to integrate personality in a majority of cases. Patients, however darkly, appear to divine this of themselves, and I have heard perhaps 50 men make this remark independently: "I see now that my drinking was only a detail. The real trouble with me was that my whole life and my thought were wrong. This is why I drank."[9]

One of the central flaws in the Emmanuel approach to the treatment of alcoholism was its heavy dependence on Freudian psychotherapy and the use of suggestion. According to Edward McKinley, "The Emmanuel workers did not realize that the 'strengthening of the will' which they observed in alcoholic patients was actually the result of the projection of their authority on the patient."[10] And Carl Rogers includes "suggestion" under "methods in dispute" in his discussion of psychotherapy. He states:

> The client is told in a variety of ways, "You're getting better," "You're doing well," "You're improving," all in the hope that it will strengthen his motivation in these directions. . . . [S]uch suggestion is essentially repressive. It denies the problem which exists, and it denies the feeling which the individual has about the problem.[11]

The Emmanuel Movement continued until 1940, the year of Elwood Worcester's death. Since the Movement no longer exists and there are no quantitative research reports on which to judge the effectiveness of its approach, it is difficult to evaluate its degree of success in breaking the addictive cycle. However, in a comparative analysis of treatment outcomes, studies indicate negative results for psychotherapy, which was a central part of the Emmanuel approach.[12]

Like the Washingtonians and the other self-help organizations that preceded it, the Emmanuel Movement experienced wide acceptance and rapid growth; but because of an inability to deal effectively with the long-term problem of relapse, it eventually experienced a slow death.

---

1. *Understanding and Counseling the Alcoholic Through Religion and Psychology*, by Howard Cinebell, Jr. New York: Abington Press, 1956, p. 87.
2. Ibid.
3. Ibid, p. 82.
4. Ibid., pp. 88–89.
5. Ibid., p. 84.
6. Ibid., p. 75.
7. *Stations of the Lost*, by Jacqueline P Wiseman. Englewood Cliffs, NJ: Prentice-Hall, 1970, p. 209.
8. Cinebell, op. cit., pp. 94–95.
9. Ibid.
10. Ibid., p. 97.
11. Ibid., p. 98.
12. Ibid., p. 107. See also *Handbook of Alcoholism Treatment Approaches (Second Edition)*, Reid Hester and William Miller, eds. Boston: Allyn & Bacon, 1995.

3

The Origins of Alcoholics Anonymous

In order to understand Alcoholics Anonymous, it is first necessary to understand the organization that gave birth to AA and made its existence possible. This was an evangelical religious movement which was initially called A First Century Christian Fellowship, later the Oxford Group Movement, and finally Moral Re-Armament. The founder of this religious movement was the Reverend Frank Nathan Daniel Buchman, who was born on June 4, 1878 in Pennsburg, Pennsylvania, the son of Franklin and Sarah Buchman. He attended Muhlenburg College in Allentown, Pennsylvania, a religious school owned and managed by the Lutheran Ministerium of Pennsylvania, whose principal purpose was to provide education for those who would become Lutheran ministers. In 1899, Buchman graduated from Muhlenburg and was accepted at the Lutheran Theological Seminary at Mount Airy in Philadelphia.

In 1901, while still in the seminary, Buchman attended an important event, the Northfield Student Conference in Massachusetts managed by John R. Mott, the Assistant General Secretary of the Young Mens Christian Association. At that time, Mott was a dominant figure in the student evangelical movement. Buchman reported afterwards that the conference "completely changed [my] life."[1] After this conference, Buchman apparently decided that world evangelism and the winning of souls for Christ would be his life's work.

After graduation from the Mount Airy seminary in 1902, Buchman worked for a year at the Church of the Good Shepherd School for the Blind in Overbrook, Pennsylvania. In 1904, he founded the Lutheran Hospice for Young Men, which was essentially a homeless shelter. Buchman became the "house father" with the blessing of the Ministerium board. The six board members expected Buchman to make the hospice self-sustaining and he was told to make fundraising a top priority. The circumstances under which the shelter operated made this virtually impossible, and in 1907 Buchman was forced to resign. Because his whole world was tied up in the hospice, this resignation put Buchman's life in emotional ruins.[2]

Years of overwork had exhausted Buchman, and his physician, Weir

Mitchell, recommended a holiday. Buchman's father gave him $1000 (roughly equivalent to $20,000 today), and he was off to Europe.[3] He toured Germany and then England, where he attended the Keswick Convention, an annual gathering of evangelical Christians.

While in Keswick, Buchman attended a religious service in a small stone church given by the evangelist Jessie Penn-Lewis. In her sermon, Penn-Lewis talked about the cross of Christ and the doctrine of atonement. This sermon so moved Buchman that it became a life-changing experience for him. As he put it:

> She pictured the dying Christ as I had never seen Him pictured before. . . . I saw the nails which held His feet. I saw the spear in His side, and I saw the look of sorrow and infinite suffering in His face. I knew that I had wounded Him, that there was a great distance between myself and Him, and I knew that it was my sin of nursing ill-will. I thought of those six men back in Philadelphia [the board members of the Lutheran Ministerium] who I felt had wronged me. They probably had, but I'd got so mixed up in the wrong that I was the seventh wrong man. . . .
>
> I began to see myself as God saw me, which was a very different picture than the one I had of myself. . . . I sat there and realized how my sin, my pride, my selfishness and my ill-will, had eclipsed me from God and Christ. I was in Christian work, I had given my life to those poor boys and many people might have said "how wonderful," but I did not have victory because I was not in touch with God. . . .
>
> . . . I was the center of my own life. That big "I" had to be crossed out. I saw my resentments against those men standing out like tombstones in my heart. I asked God to change me and He told me to put things right with them.
>
> It produced in me a vibrant feeling, as though a strong current of life had suddenly been poured into me . . .[4]

Buchman believed that this conversion experience, in the brevity of that one moment, had profoundly changed his life. In the years to follow he would find more than ample confirmation of that belief.

After this, Buchman immediately wrote letters to each of the six board members of the Lutheran Ministerium with whom he had quarreled. One of these letters still remains in the archives of the Krauth Memorial Library at Mount Airy seminary. It reads as follows:

Dear Brother Ohl—
I am writing to tell you that I have harboured an unkind feeling toward you—at times I conquered it but it always came back. Our views may differ but as brothers we must love.
I write to ask your forgiveness and to assure that I love you and trust by God's grace I shall never more speak unkindly or disparagingly of you. The lines of that hymn have been ringing in my ears—

When I survey the wondrous cross
On which the Prince of Glory died
My richest gain I count but loss
And pour contempt on all my pride.

With love
faithfully yours
Frank N.D. Buchman
July 27, 1908[5]

These letters were, in large measure, written for the emotional gratification of Buchman alone. Buchman and his followers often said that the six individuals to whom he addressed these letters "did not bother" to reply. In apparent contrast to the saintly nature of Buchman's penitence, the six Ministerium board members might seem ungracious. However, there was a simple reason for their lack of response; on the back of the letter written to Dr. Ohl, the doctor penciled the following note:

Fortunately I have found the letter . . . the like of which Mr. B says he wrote to a number of others, and got no answer. But you will notice that he gives no address. Had he done so I would surely have written. As nearly as I can make out the postmark the letter was mailed in England.[6]

Buchman was apparently not in the habit of looking for corrective feedback.
After his conversion experience at Keswick, Buchman was a changed man—a man with a mission. Upon his return to America, he obtained employment through John R. Mott at YMCA headquarters. His post was that of YMCA Secretary at Pennsylvania State College. Buchman worked 18 to 20 hours a day, dramatically increasing YMCA activities on campus with a new and highly visible program of meetings and classes. Within three years, Buchman had increased student enrollment in the YMCA from 35% to 75% of the student body.

These activities did not go unnoticed. Buchman's methods were studied and copied, and he took teams of men whom he had trained to other schools in order to spread the word of God.[7]

In 1915, Buchman left Pennsylvania State College and carried the message of world evangelism to Asia, where he continued his crusade in India and China.

In 1916, he returned to the United States and accepted a post as Extension Lecturer in Personal Evangelism at the Hartford Theological Seminary in Connecticut. Buchman was not as well received as had been expected. His rigid evangelism upset both the students and staff. Buchman made it all too clear that he viewed the existing courses taught at the seminary as theoretical and, in an evangelical sense, not vital to a fundamental religious education. As far as he was concerned, the study and memorization of theological rhetoric was not as important as the moral, religious, and spiritual needs of the individual. As a result of his preaching, many students at the seminary lost their faith, and the faculty didn't know what to do about it.[8]

In 1917, Buchman left the Hartford seminary and went to China to continue his evangelical crusade. There he helped to establish the National Society for the Salvation of China. Buchman's crusade, like those of other evangelists in China, would fail. Many Chinese were disenchanted with Christianity because of, among other things, the actions of the Versailles Peace Conference. That Conference had handed many German concessions in China to Japan (which was on the side of the Allies in WWI), despite earlier promises to the contrary. In addition, many Chinese resented Christian missionaries such as Buchman because of their condescending attitudes.

In contrast, the Russian Communists were not condescending and made a genuine and concerted attempt to understand the Chinese people. The ease with which Communism captured the hearts and minds of a great many Chinese, in spite of vast Christian missionary efforts, stunned Buchman.[9]

Buchman returned to the United States in November 1921, and in the Autumn of 1922 founded his First Century Christian Fellowship. This organization was an attempt to return evangelism to its fundamental roots and get back to the supposed beliefs, methods, and practices of the apostles.[10] After his China experience, the lines of demarcation were clearly drawn in Buchman's mind. It was a classic battle of good against evil: Buchman would fight with God against Satan as embodied in the godless Communists.

In order to accomplish his goals, Buchman needed money and power. With the establishment of his own organization, Buchman was no longer receiving a salary from any church institution. If his new Fellowship was to survive and prosper, fundraising had to be a top priority. As with his earlier projects, Buchman eagerly embraced this new challenge. He thoroughly believed that his destiny was to change the world.

The doctrine of Buchman's new group embodied religious perfectionism in the "Four Absolutes": absolute honesty; absolute purity; absolute unselfishness; and absolute love.[11] As the leader of this religious crusade, Buchman referred to himself as a "soul surgeon," and other members of his group likewise adopted the designation.[12] After conversion, members of this new movement were expected to surrender to God, undertake rigid self-examination, openly confess the nature of their sins, and make restitution to any individuals they had harmed prior to conversion. Buchman's followers were also expected to adhere to Buchman's fiat, "no pay for soul surgery." However, they were also expected to make fundraising a priority, so they accepted contributions in order to make the organization self-sustaining.[13]

In addition to the four absolutes, Buchman also prescribed the "five Cs" and the "five procedures." The five Cs consisted of confidence (in the "soul surgeon"), confession (of sins), conviction (of the evils of one's sins), conversion (to the new Buchmanite belief system), and continuance (of practice of the four absolutes, and recruitment of new members). The five procedures were to give in (surrender) to God and listen to God's directions, check (divine) guidance (with self and other group members), make restitution to those one has harmed, share for witness, and confess one's sins. Buchman's new group had many slogans, including: "Win your argument, lose your man"; "Give news, not views"; "World changing through life changing"; and "J-E-S-U-S: Just Exactly Suits Us Sinners." In addition, members were expected to devote their lives to the cause and devote a maximum amount of effort to the attainment of the movement's goals. One group member recalled how members would walk around at movement functions smiling enthusiastically and asking each other, "Are you a maximum?"[14]

Buchman's goal was "God-control" of the world, in other words, a theocracy. In his book, *The Mystery of Moral Re-Armament*, Tom Driberg states:

One of MRA's main watchwords, 'God control,' is almost precisely synonymous with the word 'theocracy'; and it is confidently asserted in MRA propaganda that when the key men—the rulers . . . enough 'top people' are Changed, the world will become controlled by God, automatically or as though by some exercise in mass-suggestion.[15]

Because of this belief in the necessity of "changing" "key men," Buchman targeted those who were in positions of wealth and political power. He desired to convert those individuals whose transformation, he believed, would most quickly affect society at large. This belief and goal was out of keeping with Buchman's background. Dr. Mahlon Hellrich, archivist at the Lehigh Valley Historical Society, viewed Buchman as an anomaly within Pennsylvania Dutch society. Lutherans were raised to be deferential to the rich and prominent; it was unheard of for a Lutheran to actively convert and "change" them in the manner that Buchman did.[16]

With Buchman at the helm, his First Century Christian Fellowship grew rapidly during the 1920s. This growth, however, was accompanied by controversy. In the Spring of 1924, Dr. John G. Hibden, President of Princeton University, banned Buchman from the university campus. Hibden stated: "As long as I am the President of the University (and I think that I speak for the whole administration) there is no place for 'Buchmanism' in Princeton."[17] What precipitated this ban was a combination of religious zeal bordering on fanaticism, persistent invasion of personal privacy, high-pressure attempts at religious conversion, obsessive preaching on sexual sin, and pressure upon students to rely upon divine guidance, which in some cases "directed" students to neglect studies, cut classes, and skip exams.

In spite of Hibden's ban, Buchmanite activities continued on campus. Two years later, the Philadelphia Society of Princeton was charged, at a student open forum, with Buchmanite activities. So widespread was the resentment and controversy over the religious conversion techniques of the Buchmanites that President Hibden appointed a nine-member board of inquiry to investigate the matter. A student questionnaire was circulated to determine student acceptance of the Buchmanites; it reported that 75% of those polled held an unfavorable opinion of Buchman's group.[18]

At about the same time as the Princeton shenanigans, Buchman was reported to have arranged a meeting in New York between himself and Queen Marie of Romania. The combination of religion and royalty was irresistible to the press. "Buchman was from then on cast as the leader of a strange and unhealthy sect, another Rasputin exploiting a brief encounter with royalty," who operated in "darkened rooms," and who was "hysterical," "erotic," and "morbid."[19] This stigma remained attached to Buchman, despite the fact that he himself had taken no direct part in the activities of the Philadelphia Society at Princeton.

Buchman and his visions for a world theocracy were, in reality, remarkably egocentric. He expected his followers to blindly follow his lead and to accept the reality of his personal religious experiences. His followers were to experience the very same "spiritual" elements in the same order that Buchman had: a conversion experience, a surrender to God, and embracement of Buchman's vision of religious perfection. It's unlikely that the Buchman followers at Princeton could have been any more zealous than Buchman himself.

In addition to being egocentric, Buchman was also thin skinned. The newspaper articles which portrayed him as leader of a religious cult disturbed him. When the term "Buchmanism" appeared in the press, he was deeply hurt. After the negative publicity surrounding the Princeton incidents, he stated, "It was like a knife through my heart." "What is Buchmanism?" he asked. "There is no such thing! We believe in making Christianity a vital force in modern life."[20]

Yet, in a very real sense, to Buchman, Buchmanism—his movement, its ideology, and its practices—was everything. It was his whole life. He never married or raised a family, and had no hobbies or interests outside of the religious movement which was his creation. All of his thoughts and actions were devoted to his crusade.

When threatened by negative publicity, Buchman's natural instinct was to go on the offensive. So in 1927, together with several university members who had supported him during the Princeton difficulties, Buchman arranged what would be the largest American "house party" to date at Lake Minnewaska, New York. (House parties were informal religious retreats for the "up and out" held in luxurious private residences or in up-scale hotels.)[21]

At about the same time, Buchman stepped up his activities in England. In 1928, the number of young men and women attending meetings became so large that Buchman's followers were forced to rent the ballroom of the Randolph Hotel, the largest hotel in Oxford, England. The organization continued to grow, but negative press coverage continued to plague Buchman and his movement. *The Daily Express* in Oxford ran a story under the headline "Revival Scenes in Oxford," with the subheads "Undergraduates' Strange New Sect" and "Prayer Meetings in a Lounge." The *Daily Express* reporter wrote:

A sensational religious revival is causing excitement, and some consternation, among Oxford undergraduates. The main focus was a group which met every Sunday evening in the private lounge of Oxford's largest hotel, and the public confession of sin has been a feature of these meetings. Such an ordeal naturally involves a violent emotional strain and, in the case of two young men of nervous temperament, the unfortunate results of their "conversion" have provoked severe comment, and are said to be attracting the attention of the university authorities.[22]

In 1929, Buchman changed the name of his organization from A First Century Christian Fellowship to the Oxford Group Movement. The name "Oxford Group" was first used in South Africa when a railway porter wrote the phrase on labels placed on windows of railroad car compartments reserved for a team of Buchmanites, most of whom were from Oxford. The South African press picked up on the label and the name stuck.[23] Subsequently Buchman made the name change official. This was in essence a public relations ploy. The centenary of The Oxford Movement, which had sought to Catholicize the Anglican Church, would arrive in 1933, and the name change to Oxford Group Movement allowed Buchman to identify himself (at least with those who weren't paying strict attention) with the Oxford Movement. The name change also made it appear that Buchman was associated with Oxford University, though he had never attended or taught at Oxford, and had no official connection with it whatsoever. But the name change evidently served Buchman's ends, and his movement used the name Oxford Group Movement for the next decade.[24]

With the new name, the Oxford Group Movement was able to circumvent negative publicity (associated with Buchman's First Century Christian Fellowship), and it continued to grow. New meetings sprang up in both Britain and America, and the organization's fortunes were waxing, both in financial and political-influence terms.

A few years after the name change, an important event took place in Akron, Ohio. James Newton, an Oxford Group member and a personal assistant to tire magnate Harvey Firestone, noticed that Firestone's son Russell was suffering from serious alcohol problems. Newton offered to provide assistance to Firestone's son and checked him into a drying-out clinic for the wealthy in New York. Following this treatment, Newton accompanied the young man to an Oxford Group Movement conference in Denver, Colorado. After Russell's surrender to God and his "conversion" experience, Newton returned with him to Akron, where Russell remained abstinent from alcohol and seemed a changed man. Firestone's family doctor referred to this apparent change as a "medical miracle."[25]

Harvey Firestone was so impressed with Newton and the Oxford Group Movement that he personally invited Buchman to Akron. In 1933, Buchman and a team of 60 "soul surgeons" arrived and, at Firestone's request, conducted a 10-day revival crusade. The activities of the group received coverage in the local press, which attracted new followers. Upon departure, Buchman and the other groupers left behind a solid and well-established core group in Akron.[26] This group, which met in the home of T. Henry Williams, an inventor of tire-making machinery, included Akron surgeon and proctologist Robert Smith, Henrietta Seiberling, daughter-in-law of Frank Seiberling, founder of Goodyear Tire and Rubber Company, and many other prominent members of Akron society. This group was typical of the type of individuals Buchman tried to, and did in fact, attract. During the 1930s, Buchman and his organization prospered, with Buchman living a lavish existence off the contributions of his many wealthy backers. This was during the Great Depression, and Buchman was criticized for his opulent lifestyle. In 1936, he responded in *Time* magazine: "Why shouldn't we stay in 'posh' hotels? Isn't God a millionaire?"[27] As the movement grew and spread through Europe, Buchman's financial base grew.

Buchman realized, however, that he could not operate in Germany in the same manner that had been possible in America and England. In Germany, house parties and group meetings were spied upon, and large, open revival meetings were out of the question. Even given this, Buchman did not perceive Hitler as a threat as late as the summer of 1936.

After a tour of Germany and a visit to the Berlin Olympics, Buchman returned to the United States. Upon his return, Buchman was interviewed by William A.H. Birnie, from the *New York World-Telegram*. The interview appeared in the August 26, 1936 issue of that paper. The headline read, "Hitler or Any Fascist Leader Controlled by God Could Cure All Ills of World, Buchman Believes."

The interview read, in part:

> To Dr. Frank Nathan Daniel Buchman, vigorous, outspoken, 58-year-old leader of the revivalist Oxford Group, the Fascist dictatorships of Europe suggest infinite possibilities for remaking the world and putting it under God control. . . .
> "I thank heaven for a man like Adolf Hitler, who built a front line of defense against the anti-Christ of Communism," he said today in his book-lined office in the annex to Calvary Church, Fourth Ave. and 21st St. . . . Of course, I don't condone everything the Nazis do—Anti-Semitism? Bad naturally. I suppose Hitler sees a Karl Marx in every Jew. . . . But think what it would mean to the world if Hitler surrendered to the control of God. Or Mussolini. Or any dictator. Through such a man God could control a nation overnight and solve every last, bewildering problem. . . . The world needs the dictatorship of the living spirit of God.[28]

The interview continued with Buchman stating that "Hitler is Christianity's defender against Communism."[29] Thus it wasn't surprising that from 1936 on Buchman was attacked by Radio Moscow.[30] Ironically, he was also reportedly condemned in reports by the Gestapo.

According to Buchman's MRA biographer, Garth Lean, in 1937 the Gestapo tightened surveillance of the Oxford Group; it also demanded that

German citizens involved with the Movement sever all ties with it. In 1939, the Gestapo made public a 126-page document which condemned Buchman, and it subsequently forbade German military officers to associate with the Oxford Group under any name.[31] One strongly suspects that this was due to Buchman's insistence that his followers submit to "God control," a position that would have quite probably struck German fascists as being contrary to the principle that all power must reside in Hitler and the Nazi Party.

Eventually, Buchman reportedly conceded his mistake to a group of friends: "Hitler fooled me. I thought it [Nazism] would be a bulwark against Communism."[32] He never, though, issued a public retraction of his statements in the *World-Telegram* interview.

After that notorious 1936 newspaper interview, Buchman came under increasing criticism in the press. In 1939, his organization changed its name from the Oxford Group Movement to Moral Re-Armament. He also went on the offensive, staging a major public relations event in New York City, renting Madison Square Garden for May 14, 1939. Mayor LaGuardia declared May 7–14 "MRA Week." The event succeeded, and similar gatherings were held in other cities.[33]

Buchman's Moral Re-Armament strategy was a success—at least it helped restore him briefly to a place in the sun. In 1940, Senator Harry Truman read a message from President Roosevelt to the Senate: "The underlying strength of the world must consist in the moral fiber of her citizens. A program of moral re-armament, to be most highly effective, must receive support on a worldwide scale." The press picked up on this, with the *Washington Post*, for example, running the headline, "First Anniversary Finds Moral Re-Armament World Force.[34]

Although Moral Re-Armament activities continued during World War II, the organization quickly faded from public view, except for a few very unfavorable articles condemning it for attempts by its "lay evangelists" to avoid the draft. After the war, Buchman continued his religious-moral crusade, as well as his crusade against Communism. Moral Re-Armament was an ultra-right, conservative organization, and the Cold War provided fertile soil for the seeds of its anti-Communist rhetoric.

During the years when Senator Joseph McCarthy made headlines with his infamous list of supposed Communist Party members working in the U.S. State Department, Buchman helped fuel the fears of the nation. In his crusade, Buchman denounced Communism and homosexuality, in the process abetting McCarthy and other Cold Warriors in ruining many careers and lives. Buchman continued his Cold War crusade until his death in 1961.

That crusade continued after his death. In 1964, Buchman's successor as head of MRA, Peter Howard, wrote in his book, *Britain and the Beast,* that "[a]t one point, 264 homosexuals were reported to have been purged from the American State Department. Many of them moved from Washington to New York and took jobs with the United Nations . . ."[35] This startling information was contained in a chapter titled "Queens and Queers."

Despite its unsavory political activities, MRA was at heart a religious movement. Author Charles S. Braden describes part of the nature of Buchman's movement:

> One does not have to leave his own church to become a member of the Oxford Group Movement. Rather it was an attempt to intensify religious devotion and to make it function within the church. Perhaps the most insistent emphasis of the movement has been its emphasis upon what used to be called "personal work," that is the winning of individual souls.[36]

Although Buchman himself had access to wealth, organizationally his movement had no tangible assets until relatively late in its existence. Until 1941, the headquarters of the movement in America had been housed in the Rev. Samuel Shoemaker's Calvary Episcopal Church. After Shoemaker broke from Buchman and abandoned Moral Re-Armament, Buchman was forced to find other housing for his office.[37] Following the war, however, wealthy backers donated resorts in Caux, Switzerland and Mackinac Island, Michigan to MRA. So, MRA's fortunes revived somewhat, but its focus had shifted from "personal evangelism" to mass outreach in the media. In the post-war period, MRA issued a steady stream of extreme right-wing, gay-baiting books and pamphlets, of which the Peter Howard book mentioned above is but one example.

Because of its loose and intangible organizational structure, and the essentially dictatorial control of the organization by its guru, the death of Frank Buchman effectively meant the end of Moral Re-Armament. To a large extent, Buchman *was* Moral Re-Armament. (MRA continues to exist, but only as a shadow of what it was under Buchman.)

Buchman's notion of divine guidance and his failure to consider social, economic, and psychological factors formed the basis for the pronounced anti-intellectualism of his movement. To Buchman, God-control was the answer to all of the world's problems. To him, any other option was inconceivable. So, Buchman devoted his entire adult life to a bid to impose theocracy upon the world, to place all of humanity under "God-control."

Buchman's MRA biographer, Garth Lean, comments:

No sane person looking round the world in 1961, when Buchman died at the age of 83, would have described that bid as successful. On the other hand it would be equally hard to judge his life as a failure. Some remarkable streams of events sprang from his initiatives; others are still breaking surface today. It is at least arguable that few of them would have emerged if his aim had been smaller.[38]

The most prominent of the "stream of events" that "sprang from [Buchman's] intitiatives" is Alcoholics Anonymous.

---

1. *On the Tail of a Comet*, by Garth Lean. Colorado Springs, CO: Helmers and Howard Publishers, 1988, p. 17.
2. Ibid., p. 63.
3. Ibid., pp. 25–28.
4. Ibid., p. 28.
5. *The Mystery of Moral Re-Armament*, by Tom Driberg. New York: Alfred A. Knopf, 1965, p. 36.
6. Ibid, p. 37.
7. Lean, op. cit., pp. 33–34.
8 Ibid., pp. 49–50.
9. Ibid., pp. 45–72.
10. Ibid., p. 97.
11. Driberg, op. cit., p. 32.
12. *Getting Better Inside Alcoholics Anonymous*, by Nan Robertson. New York: Wm. Morrow, 1988, p. 58.
13. *Dr. Bob and the Good Oldtimers*, author unknown. New York: Alcoholics Anonymous World Services, 1980, p. 54.
14. Ibid., p. 55.
15. Driberg, op. cit., p. 22
16. Lean, op. cit., p. 99.
17. Driberg, op. cit., p. 61.
18. Ibid., pp. 61–63.
19. Lean, op. cit., p. 125.
20. Ibid.
21. Ibid., p. 134.
22. Driberg, op. cit., pp. 52–53.
23. *Alcoholics Anonymous: Cult or Cure?*, by Charles Bufe. San Francisco: See Sharp Press, 1991, p. 21.
24. Lean, op. cit., p. 151.
25. *Pass It On*, author unknown. New York: Alcoholics Anonymous World Services, 1984, pp. 136–137.
26. Bufe, op. cit., p. 18.
27. Driberg, op. cit., pp. 68–72.
28. Ibid, p. 72.
29. Lean, op. cit., p. 1.
30. Ibid., pp. 240–242.
31. Ibid, p. 241.

32. Ibid, p. 284.
33. Ibid.
34. Ibid., p. 285.
35. *Britain and the Beast*, by Peter Howard. London: Heinemann, 1963, p. 47.
36. *These Also Believe: A Study of Modern American Cults and Minority Religious Movements*, by Charles S. Braden. New York: Macmillan, 1949, p. 403.
37. Ibid., p. 413.
38. Lean, op. cit., p. 1.

4

Bill Wilson
Co-Founder of Alcoholics Anonymous

William Griffith ("Bill") Wilson, the "more equal" of Alcoholics Anonymous' co-founders, was born on November 26, 1895 in East Dorset, Vermont. He was the son of Gilman Wilson and Emily Griffith Wilson. In 1906, Emily divorced Gilman because of Gilman's heavy drinking. At the turn of the century, such a separation was unheard of in small New England towns, and scandal resulted. William and his younger sister Dorothy felt abandoned, shamed, and disgraced as a result of the divorce, and they felt inferior to the other children in the community, who lived with both parents. Perhaps as a result, Bill suffered one of the first of his many depressions for almost a year following his parents' separation. He missed his father deeply and would not see him again for nine years. He was to suffer further feelings of abandonment when his mother moved away to attend college to pursue and ultimately achieve a successful career in medicine as an osteopath.[1]

In 1918, Bill Wilson married Lois Burnham, moved to New York City, and after taking and losing several other jobs began a career as a Wall Street securities analyst and margin trader. He also followed in his father's footsteps as a heavy drinker. Following the stock market crash in 1929, in which he lost nearly everything, his drinking grew worse. In 1933, he checked himself into Towns Hospital, a drying-out facility; this was to be the first of four stays at Towns. His final stay began on December 11, 1934. A physician at the facility, Dr. Leonard Silkworth, sedated him and began administering a cocktail of belladonna and other drugs. (Belladonna is an atropine powder derived from the leaves and roots of *Atropa belladonna*, a poisonous and highly toxic Eurasian plan commonly referred to as "deadly nightshade.")

What happened after administration of the drugs can be described best in Wilson's own words:

My depression deepened unbearably and finally it seemed to me as though I were at the bottom of a pit. I still gagged badly on the notion of a Power greater than myself, but finally, just for the moment, the last vestige of my proud obstinacy was crushed. All at once I found myself crying out, "If there is a God, let Him show Himself! I am ready to do anything, anything."

Suddenly the room lit up with a great white light. I was caught up into an ecstasy which there are no words to describe. It seemed to me, in my mind's eye, that I was on a mountain and that a wind not of air but of spirit was blowing. And then it burst upon me that I was a free man. Slowly the ecstasy subsided. I lay on the bed, but for a time I was in another world, a new world of consciousness. All about me and through me was a wonderful feeling of Presence, and I thought to myself, "So this is the God of the preachers!"[2]

Nan Robertson, in her book, *Getting Better Inside Alcoholics Anonymous*, suggests that this deep religious experience might have been the result of hallucinations during Wilson's withdrawal from alcohol, or might have been induced or precipitated by his medication.[3] In any event, his psychic conversion was accomplished. On the surface at least, he was a changed man. But he apparently was never able to re-experience his original "spiritual awakening," which in later years he would call his "hot flash," though he continued to seek some form of spiritual transformation. After being discharged from the hospital, Wilson began a crusade to religiously convert and save other alcoholics, and began to regularly attend Oxford Group meetings.[4]

Wilson's conversion experience kept him sober for five months. Then, while on business in Akron, Ohio, he was overcome by the fear of relapse, and he panicked. He went to a telephone booth, turned to the church directory, and called the Reverend Walter Tunks. Wilson explained his situation to Tunks and said that he needed to talk with another alcoholic in order to maintain sobriety. Tunks supplied Wilson with several names. Finally, Wilson contacted Henrietta Seiberling, who arranged a meeting with Dr. Robert Smith, who was also a heavy drinker. The two men had what has been subsequently described as the first AA meeting.[5]

But Alcoholics Anonymous was the result of more than just a hot flash and a chance encounter. Not only Wilson, but Tunks, Seiberling, and Dr. Smith were all Oxford Group members. As well, both Smith and Wilson were native Vermonters who came from relatively privileged backgrounds, and the two men struck up an immediate friendship. Wilson became Smith's house guest during the summer of 1935, while the two men attempted to save other drunks through converting them to Oxford Group principles (God-control, making amends, confession, etc.).

Upon his return to New York, Wilson maintained contact with Smith, who was using his position at City Hospital in Akron to apply Oxford

Group principles in a medical setting. In New York, Wilson continued his active involvement in the Oxford Group Movement through the Reverend Sam Shoemaker and Calvary Episcopal Church, which at the time was the American headquarters of Frank Buchman and his movement.

Aside from Oxford Group literature and preachings, Wilson and Smith were at sea as to how to proceed. They had never heard of the Washingtonians and had at best vague ideas about the temperance movement. Thus it's not surprising that they relied very heavily upon Oxford Group ideology and procedures in their attempts to help other drunks. Nan Robertson quotes Smith as saying, "We were groping in the dark. I, a physician, knew nothing about [alcoholism] to speak of. There wasn't anything worth reading in the textbooks. Usually the information consisted of some queer treatments for the DTs, if the patient had gone that far. If he hadn't, you prescribed a few bromides and gave the fellow a good lecture."[6]

Thus when AA started, its founders knew nothing about 19th-century self-help movements—even though some, such as the Sons of Temperance, were similar in some ways to AA—and they were apparently entirely unaware of the work of the Medical Association for the Study of Inebriety and Narcotics and its publication, the *Journal of Inebriety*, which had ceased publication in 1914.

The American temperance movement and the prohibition period which it helped to bring about had indeed created a vacuum within the medical community as regards addiction treatment. Alcoholics Anonymous came into being at a time when modern methods of medical therapy, clinical psychology, clinical sociology, and professional counseling were virtually nonexistent in the field. AA, through default, filled this near vacuum. Because it was the first organization to gain a toe-hold in this area, AA would, again through default, obtain the franchise on, and eventually a monopoly position within, the recovery movement. The near vacuum, however, was just that—a near vacuum, not a total vacuum. As we saw in Chapter 2, there were organizations which did deal with alcoholics at the time AA came about: the Salvation Army and the Emmanuel Movement.

While it is doubtful that either Bill Wilson or Dr. Bob Smith knew of the Emmanuel Movement, they might have been aware of the Salvation Army's work, so it appears peculiar that they apparently made no attempt to research such approaches. But this only appears to be peculiar. Bill Wilson had quite literally "seen the light." His vision of recovery from alcoholism embraced one thing and one thing only: religious conversion. To Wilson, research wasn't necessary; religion was The Answer. And when one has The Answer, research and questioning are obstacles, not aids. The problem is not finding new, better approaches, but rather putting an end to questions so that The Answer can be adopted without opposition.

To Wilson and Smith, recovery was a matter of faith, not a matter of research and hard evidence. Taking this approach, Wilson and Smith seized upon Frank Buchman's Oxford Group Movement, with its extreme emphasis on personal powerlessness and reliance upon divine guidance, as the answer to alcoholism. (This answer, not incidentally, had a powerful anti-intellectual aspect, an aspect which is still a prominent feature of con-temporary AA.) AA's co-founders viewed hospitals, doctors, and psychi-atrists as ineffective in dealing with alcoholism. This seems ironic given that one of them (Smith) was an MD, but he, like Wilson, believed that the only cure for alcoholism was through God; and he used hospitalization of alcoholism patients not for medical treatment, but rather so that they could be isolated and indoctrinated into Oxford Group Movement/AA beliefs. Wilson and Smith did not perceive their lack of scientific knowledge as an impediment, as they considered such knowledge irrelevant.

Perhaps not so curiously, given that all had religious roots, AA evolved to be similar in many ways to its 19th-century predecessors, the Washing-tonian Society and the self-help organizations associated with the temper-ance movement. As well, AA in institutional form, as embodied in the "Minnesota Model" of 12-step treatment, would become very similar to the Emmanuel Movement. Had Wilson and Smith been more critically minded, and had they been aware of the existence and history of AA's predecessors, they might have done things quite differently—given that all of AA's predecessors ultimately failed.

Wilson remained within the confines of the Oxford Group Movement for more than two years following his meeting with Smith and their early attempts to save other alcoholics; and Smith and his group in Akron stayed within the Oxford Groups for four years following that meeting.

After his return to New York in 1935, Wilson had turned his home into a halfway house for alcoholics and began holding Oxford Group meetings there exclusively for alcoholics. Although the followers who met at Wilson's home also attended regular Oxford Group meetings, they found the latter too authoritarian and were made to feel less than welcome by some of the nonalcoholic members.

In addition, Buchman was a very high profile and controversial person. Many of his views alienated the Catholic as well as the Jewish community. The August 26, 1936 interview in the *New York World-Telegram* con-taining Buchman's famous quote, "I thank heaven for a man like Adolf Hitler," might well have frightened Wilson. Wilson wanted to remain apolitical and to avoid controversy in order to concentrate on alcoholism. This desire coupled with the friction between Wilson's alcoholics and the nonalcoholic Oxford Group members led to Wilson's New York group severing formal relations with the Oxford Group Movement in 1937.[7]

AA's Message

AA's philosophy was taken directly from the Oxford Group Movement. Frank Buchman's beliefs in human powerlessness, the necessity of confession of sin, the value of taking a moral inventory of oneself, the value of making amends to others, the necessity of "carrying the message" to others, and redemption through turning one's life over to God were adopted wholesale by Bill Wilson. Wilson simply took these central Buchmanite principles and formatted them into the 12-step "program of recovery" from alcoholism—a "program of recovery" that mentions alcohol and alcoholics only twice (in the first and twelfth steps). Wilson's codification of Oxford Group principles reads as follows:

1. We admitted we were powerless over alcohol—that our lives had become unmanageable.
2. Came to believe that a Power greater than ourselves could restore us to sanity.
3. Made a decision to turn our will and our lives over to the care of God as we understood Him.
4. Made a searching and fearless moral inventory of ourselves.
5. Admitted to God, to ourselves, and to another human being the exact nature of our wrongs.
6. Were entirely ready to have God remove all these defects of character.
7. Humbly asked Him to remove our shortcomings.
8. Made a list of all persons we had harmed, and became willing to make amends to them all.
9. Made direct amends to such people wherever possible, except when to do so would injure them or others.
10. Continued to take personal inventory and when we were wrong promptly admitted it.
11. Sought through prayer and meditation to improve our conscious contact with God as we understood Him, praying only for knowledge of His will for us and the power to carry that out.
12. Having had a spiritual awakening as the result of these steps, we tried to carry this message to alcoholics, and to practice these principles in all our affairs.[8]

Beyond the wholesale adoption of Oxford Group principles, Bill Wilson's vision of a recovery program was remarkably egocentric. As we shall see, the basic concepts of his program mirrored the parochial singularities of his own recovery experience. The first concept is that of "hitting bottom." Within AA, hitting bottom or reaching a state of total emotional collapse and depression—as Wilson had—is viewed as an essential component to the recovery process.

The second, related concept within the program is "deflation of ego in depth." This is essentially the admission and acceptance of defeat. Desperation is thus viewed as another essential component of recovery. In Bill Wilson's view, "proud obstinacy" had to be "crushed," and desperation was necessary to a conversion experience. So, the program in essence requires a leap of faith.

The third concept is that of a "higher power." After "hitting bottom" and having one's ego crushed, it is essential that one turn one's life and will over to an external entity which is more powerful and more capable of managing one's life than oneself. So, Wilson's recovery program entailed psychic surrender, surrender of self-direction; one had to turn one's life and will over to "the God of the preachers," or at least to the belief system of AA.

The Big Book

The "Big Book," *Alcoholics Anonymous,* like the 12 steps within it, is a codification of Oxford Group beliefs,[9] and is for all intents and purposes AA's Bible. In its first printing, the book's title page describes its contents as "The Story of How More Than One Hundred Men Have Recovered From Alcoholism." In January 1939, "One Hundred Men" was even the working title of the book. However, a group member named Florence R., the only woman in the group at the time, objected to the title, and the name fell by the wayside. Her story in the first edition was titled, "A Feminine Victory." (She later relapsed into active alcoholism and died of an apparent suicide in Washington, DC.) "Alcoholics Anonymous" became the title of the book as well as the name of the new organization.[10]

While the text portion of *Alcoholics Anonymous* was drawn wholesale from the Oxford Group Movement, the stories in the book had a consistent theme and pattern which helped reinforce the preachings in the text portion of the book: prior to alcohol consumption, life had been normal; alcohol had taken over the writer's life and caused great misery; abstinence achieved through AA and its 12-step program had saved the writer's life and wonderfully transformed it. (This message is remarkably reminiscent of that of the Washingtonians, and one can still hear it regularly at AA speaker meetings.)

With its publication in 1939, the Big Book and the 12 steps became the core of the AA program. In the book, Wilson eliminated the Oxford Group's Four Absolutes and Five Cs, and replaced them with the 12 steps.[11] AA as a whole eventually dropped the use of Oxford Group literature and the Bible at meetings, replacing them with AA's own "inspired" text, the Big Book.

In fact, although Wilson had severed relations with the Oxford Group Movement, Oxford Group literature continued to be used at AA meetings for more than a decade after AA formally separated from the OGM. In 1948, "Dr. Bob" recalled that the Oxford Groups' "four absolutes" were "the only yardsticks" AA had in the early days, before the 12 steps:

> Almost always, if I measure my decision carefully by the yardsticks of absolute honesty, absolute unselfishness, absolute purity, and absolute love, and it checks up pretty well with those four, then my answer can't be very much out of the way. The absolutes are still published and widely quoted at A.A. meetings in the Akron-Cleveland area.[12]

The Twelve Traditions

In 1946, Wilson formulated and published the Twelve Traditions of Alcoholics Anonymous. Just as the 12 steps were written as guidelines for individual AA members, the 12 traditions were to serve as operational guidelines for the organization as a whole. Although published in the AA periodical, *The Grapevine*, in 1946, the traditions were not officially adopted until July 1950 at AA's first international convention. They read as follows.

1. Our common welfare should come first; personal recovery depends upon A.A. unity.
2. For our group purpose there is but one ultimate authority—a loving God as He may express Himself in our group conscience. Our leaders are but trusted servants; they do not govern.
3. The only requirement for A.A. membership is a desire to stop drinking.
4. Each group should be autonomous except in matters affecting other groups or A.A. as a whole.
5. Each group has but one primary purpose—to carry the message to the alcoholic who still suffers.
6. An A.A. group ought never endorse, finance, or lend the A.A. name to any related facility or outside enterprise, lest problems of money, property, and prestige divert us from our primary purpose.
7. Every A.A. group ought to be fully self-supporting, declining outside contributions.
8. Alcoholics Anonymous should remain forever nonprofessional, but our service centers may employ special workers.
9. A.A. as such, ought never be organized; but we may create service boards or committees directly responsible to those they serve.

10. Alcoholics Anonymous has no opinion on outside issues; hence the A.A. name ought never be drawn into public controversy.
11. Our public relations policy is based on attraction rather than promotion; we need always maintain personal anonymity at the level of the press, radio, and films.
12. Anonymity is the spiritual foundation of our traditions, ever reminding us to place principles before personalities.[13]

Although AA's origins and principles were religious, Wilson referred to AA as "spiritual." He did this, presumably, to avoid conflicts with established religions and to make clear to potential members that they would not have to change religious affiliations. Even today, AA members continue to insist that AA is "spiritual, not religious," even though probably a good majority of them believe that the 12 steps and Big Book were "inspired" by God, and even though religious practices such as prayer, public confession, and witnessing are a staple at AA meetings. As well, AA philosophy maintains that only a spiritual-religious "conversion experience" and turning one's life over to God (euphemistically, "a Higher Power") can effectively conquer the "disease" of alcoholism.

Wilson's recovery program also maintains that once an individual is an alcoholic, permanent abstinence coupled with lifelong attendance at AA meetings is the only effective way to deal with the "illness." Members are also told that they will have to embrace the practices of AA "one day at a time" for the rest of their lives, and that they will have to embrace the AA program as a permanent pattern of living, "the AA way of life." The only alternatives are "jails, institutions, or death."

AA members routinely present the 12-step approach to newcomers (and to each other) as infallible. Bill Wilson was largely responsible for this:

We need to ask ourselves but one short question. "Do I now believe, or am I willing to believe, that there is a power greater than myself?" As soon as a man can say that he does believe, or is willing to believe, we empathetically assure him that he is on his way. It has been repeatedly proven among us that upon this simple cornerstone a wonderfully effective spiritual structure can be built.[14]

Wilson went on:

Rarely have we seen a person fail who has thoroughly followed our path. Those who do not recover are people who cannot or will not completely give themselves to this simple program . . . [15]

AA slogans, such as "Keep coming back. It works!" and "It works if you work it," reinforce the perception that AA's program is infallible, that it *always* works for those who really try.

Bill Wilson as a Model of Recovery

In many ways, it's odd that Bill Wilson has been presented as a recovery role model. Nan Robertson correctly notes that, "The only world in which Wilson succeeded was the world of Alcoholics Anonymous."[16] AA sheltered him from the demands of nine-to-five employment, which would have required punctual and consistent job attendance and performance— things which would have been very difficult for Wilson. According to Robertson, "His moods could swing violently, from extreme optimism to despair. Beginning at age seventeen, he suffered crippling bouts of depression. The final and most prolonged came on a decade after he became sober, and went on for eleven years, until 1955."[17]

These depressive periods were a lifelong problem, and Wilson was treated for them by psychiatrists Harry Tiebout and Frances Weeks, apparently without much success. Marty Mann, an early AA member and founder of the AA front group, the National Committee for Education on Alcoholism (now the National Council on Alcoholism and Drug Dependence), said: "It was awful. There were long periods of time when he couldn't get out of bed. He just stayed in bed, and Lois [Wilson] would see that he ate. An awful lot of people believed he was drinking. That was one of the worst rumors within A.A."[18]

Nell Wing, Wilson's secretary from 1950 until his death, said: "He would come down to the office many times and sit across from me and just put his head in his hands and not really be able to communicate, just almost weep."[19] The former general manager of AA's General Service Office also confirmed Wilson's depressive tendencies: "There were some times when these horrible depressions would go on and on, for days and days. Then it was pretty hard to make contact with him. He'd try and cooperate if you had a question, but to try and sit down and do any planning with him at that time was useless."[20]

While in the midst of his severe 11-year depression, Wilson wrote *Twelve Steps and Twelve Traditions*, his guide to working the steps and to becoming "happily and usefully whole." This book, like the Big Book, would prove a major financial boon to Wilson. Before his death, he received hundreds of thousands of dollars from AA in royalty payments, and since his death his heirs have received literally millions—probably tens of millions—in royalty payments.[21]

Truly, AA was the one thing that Bill Wilson succeeded at.

Wilson's LSD Experiments

Throughout his life, Bill Wilson sought to recapture the "hot flash" he had experienced at Towns Hospital in 1934. In the winter of 1943–44, Wilson met Aldous Huxley, author of *The Doors of Perception* (which dealt with psychedelic experiences), and the two men became friends. Through Huxley, Wilson was introduced to Dr. Humphrey Osmond and Dr. Abraham Hoffer, who were working with alcoholics and schizophrenics in a mental hospital in Canada. In 1954, Osmond and Hoffer began experimenting with LSD in their clinical treatments, and during the mid 1950s Osmond and Hoffer began administering a combination of LSD and mescaline to their patients. These treatments produced a profound psychic reaction which was similar in nature and scope to Wilson's conversion experience at Towns Hospital. Initial treatment reports were positive, and Wilson became interested when he heard of the two psychiatrists' results.

Nan Robertson quotes Wilson's secretary, Nell Wing, as stating: "Bill wanted to see what it was like. He was intrigued with the work that Osmond and Hoffer were doing in Saskatoon with alcoholics. . . . That's why he took it [LSD] himself. He had an experience [that] was totally spiritual, [like] his initial spiritual experience."[22]

Wilson was enthusiastic about LSD; he believe that it eliminated ego barriers that stood in the way of direct contact with the cosmos and God. He invited many of his associates to experiment with him, and even convinced his wife Lois to try the drug. Wilson continued using LSD until 1959. When the news of his drug experimentation became public, it scandalized many in AA, who were violently opposed to the use of any mind-altering drugs. The public exposure and pressure from within AA forced him to discontinue using it. Reports of psychotic reactions caused the Canadian government to officially ban LSD in 1963, and its until-then producer, Sandoz Pharmaceuticals, discontinued its marketing and production in that same year.[23]

Bill Wilson and Niacin

Although the LSD experiments had ended, Wilson kept in contact with Osmond and Hoffer. Following discontinuation of the LSD studies, they turned to another, nonpsychoactive chemical: niacin, a B vitamin. Osmond and Hoffer believed that they were having successful results treating alcoholics with niacin, and that they could also be successful treating schizophrenics with vitamin therapy.

In the Big Book, Wilson's friend Dr. Silkworth states that alcoholism is an "allergy." Wilson believed that Osmond and Hoffer had discovered the "exact nature" of that "allergy," and he began experimenting with megavitamin therapy. He began to publicly promote the practice in 1967. Just as Wilson's LSD experimentation had scandalized many in AA, his advocacy of megavitamin therapy also shocked many AA members. In promoting this treatment, Wilson had violated two of AA's traditions, six and ten (see pp. 57–58), by endorsing an "outside enterprise" and by drawing AA (through himself, as AA's co-founder) into "public controversy." However, there was no way for AA to prevent Wilson from engaging in megavitamin therapy or from promoting it; the only thing that AA as an organization could do was to ensure that Wilson did not use the AA name or its facilities in his promotional efforts.

Bill Wilson's Fatal Addiction

One habit in which Bill Wilson engaged almost until his death was smoking cigarettes. He was a chain smoker and hopelessly addicted to tobacco. Although he attempted to quit as early as 1940, he was never able to do so. During the mid 1960s, he developed emphysema and began to carry a pocket inhaler; yet he continued to smoke. He died in 1971 from emphysema.

In spite of Wilson's fatal tobacco addiction, his recurrent, debilitating depressions, and the scandal caused by his LSD experimentation and megavitamin advocacy, Alcoholics Anonymous grew during his lifetime to the point where it effectively monopolized the recovery movement and the field of addictions treatment within the United States and Canada. And AA members continue to revere Bill Wilson as a model (if not *the* model) of successful recovery.

---

1. *Pass It On*, no author listed. New York: Alcoholics Anonymous World Services, 1984, pp. 13–27.
2. *Alcoholics Anonymous Comes of Age*, by Bill Wilson. New York: Alcoholics Anonymous World Services, 1957, p. 63.
3. *Getting Better Inside Alcoholics Anonymous*, by Nan Robertson. New York, Wm. Morrow and Co., 1988, p. 140.
4. Wilson, op. cit., p. 64.
5. *Dr. Bob and the Good Oldtimers*, no author listed. New York: Alcoholics Anonymous World Services, 1980, pp. 63–67.
6. Robertson, op. cit., pp. 56–57.
7. *Alcoholics Anonymous Comes of Age*, op. cit., pp. 74–75.
8. Ibid., p. 50.

9. See *Alcoholics Anonymous: Cult or Cure (Second Edition)*, by Charles Bufe. Tucson, AZ: See Sharp Press, 1998, chapters 4 and 5; see also *Resisting 12-Step Coercion: How to Fight Forced Participation in AA, NA, or 12-Step Treatment*, by Stanton Peele, Charles Bufe, and Archie Brodsky. Tucson, AZ: See Sharp Press, 2000, chapter 3.
10. *Pass It On*, op. cit., pp. 202–203.
11. See Bufe, op. cit., chapters 4 and 5; see also Peele et al., op. cit., p. 103.
12. *Dr. Bob and the Good Oldtimers*, op. cit., p. 55.
13. *Twelve Steps and Twelve Traditions*, by Bill Wilson. New York: Alcoholics Anonymous World Services, 1953, pp. 133–192.
14. *Alcoholics Anonymous*, by Bill Wilson. New York: Alcoholics Anonymous World Services, 1976, p. 47.
15. Ibid., p. 58.
16. Robertson, op. cit., p. 38.
17. Ibid., p. 37.
18. *Pass It On*, op. cit., p. 293.
19. Ibid.
20. Ibid.
21. See Robertson, op. cit., pp. 83–84.
22. *Pass It On*, op. cit., p. 370.
23. Ibid., pp. 375–377.

5

The Growth of AA and the 12-Step Movement

In 1937, when Bill Wilson and his followers broke away from the Oxford Group Movement (OGM) in New York City, the unnamed organization had about 40 members.[1] In 1939, when Dr. Bob Smith and the Akron group separated from the OGM, the newly named group Alcoholics Anonymous had at least twice that total, in Akron, Cleveland, and New York.[2] So, during its first four years, AA increased from two members to roughly 100.

After publication of *Alcoholics Anonymous*, Wilson and the other AA members expected AA membership to increase drastically. This didn't happen. Following publication of the Big Book, 5000 copies sat on the shelves of a warehouse for months. Wilson and his fellow AAs thought that publicity was the answer, and a relatively new member named Morgan R. supplied the first burst of it. Prior to his alcoholic decline, he had been a successful advertising executive and he still maintained influential contacts within the industry. One such contact was Gabriel Heatter, who hosted a popular national radio program called "We the People." Heatter specialized in human-interest interviews, followed by commentary, in the manner of today's late-night talk shows. The type of publicity possible through Heatter would, Morgan and the other AA members believed, be of immense help to the fledgling organization. Morgan gave a sales pitch for AA, and Heatter booked him. He scheduled Morgan for an interview on April 25, 1939 at 9:00 p.m.

Upon hearing of the upcoming interview, Wilson and the other AAs became both excited and concerned. When Harvey Firestone invited Frank Buchman and other OGM members to Akron to establish a chapter of the organization there, it was because the Oxford Group had supposedly cured his son Russell of alcoholism. After news of this "medical miracle" reached the public, the Akron chapter initially prospered. However, after the young Firestone relapsed and returned to his old alcoholic behavior, Oxford Group support declined dramatically in Akron.[3] Wilson and the other group members were very much aware of this situation. Also, Morgan had only recently been released from the Greystone Asylum for the Insane, and the possibility of his relapsing was a real worry. It was decided that continuous surveillance of the reluctant Morgan would be necessary for a week prior to the interview. A double room was booked in Manhattan's Downtown Athletic Club, and AA members guarded Morgan 24 hours a day until the appointed time.

Bill Wilson recalled:

> An hour before broadcast time, our whole membership and their families gathered about their radios to wait for the great moment. Sighs of relief went up in every New York member's home when Morgan's voice was heard. He had hit the deadline without getting drunk. It was a heart-stirring three minutes.[4]

The interview, though, did not generate the response that Wilson and the other AA members expected. AA as an organization would have to struggle for two additional years before getting the publicity break that would dramatically increase membership.

That break came in the form of a feature article written by Jack Alexander in the March 1, 1941 issue of the *Saturday Evening Post,* at the time one of the most important American magazines. Alexander presented a very positive image of Alcoholics Anonymous, complete with photographs. The article produced the results that Wilson and company had expected from the Heatter interview. Mail and telegram inquiries deluged AA, and book sales increased dramatically. The 1941 year-end report compiled by AA secretaries placed total membership at 8000.[5]

In 1949, AA was recognized by the American Psychiatric Association, which gave Wilson credibility, and additional favorable articles from an almost entirely uncritical press spurred further growth. During AA's first quarter century (counting the time AA was formally a part of the Oxford Groups), not a single critical article appeared in any national publication indexed by the *Reader's Guide to Periodical Literature*, while there were numerous laudatory articles.

AA grew rapidly through its first half century, especially in the 1970s and 1980s, and by 1990 had 900,000 members in the United States. AA growth slowed significantly in the early 1990s, with the decline of the 12-step inpatient treatment industry, and was essentially flat by the mid 1990s. AA currently (December 2000) claims a U.S. membership of 1.16 million, a figure which has been remarkably stable over the past several years; and AA claims a current world membership of two million.[6]

Growth of Other 12-Step Groups

But it wasn't only AA that was growing during the latter part of the 20th century. Beginning in the early 1950s, 12-step movement growth would also come as a result of lateral expansion. In 1951, Al-Anon, the second 12-step organization, was founded. Al-Anon provides a network of support groups for the friends and family of alcoholics, and it follows the same 12-step philosophy as AA. In 1953, Narcotics Anonymous was founded to provide a 12-step format and a network of support groups for recovering drug addicts. Then, primarily in the 1970s and 1980s, an explosion of 12-step groups occurred, encompassing just about any compulsive or self-defeating behavior imaginable. It's significant that essentially all of these groups adopted their programs virtually unaltered from AA. In all other 12-step groups of any significant size, no matter what the problem addressed, the 12 steps are still the center of the program, and only single terms in the first and twelfth steps are changed; the other steps are unaltered.

In 1983, author-therapist Janet Geringer Woititz's book appeared, *Adult Children of Alcoholics*, which described the syndrome associated with individuals raised in an alcoholic family. This book became a best seller. After this, a series of books appeared describing the ACoA syndrome and the "codependence" syndrome. Both the ACoA and codependence movements fit within the 12-step framework, and both grew rapidly, gaining considerable media attention.[7]

Author-therapist Anne Wilson Schaef, in her 1986 book, *Codependence Mistreated-Misunderstood*, together with others in the addictions field, greatly expanded the concept of codependence from its original restrictive meaning, involving the spouse of an alcoholic. Schaef stated that "the majority of the population of the United States" suffers from codependence.[8] Others went even further. Herbert Gravitz and Julie Bowden prefaced their 1987 book, *Recovery: A Guide for Adult Children of Alcoholics*, with the statement: "Children of alcoholics are but a visible tip of a much larger social iceberg which casts an invisible shadow over as much as 96% of the population."[9]

In the Winter 1992 edition of *Contemporary Drug Problems*, an article by Robin Room, Vice-President for Research and Development at the Addiction Research Foundation, described the growth of the 12-step movement. Room's article, "Healing Ourselves and Our Planet," described the manner in which many individuals within the 12-step movement, particularly in Northern California, moved between 12-step programs for a variety of life problems, and discussed the potential for the emergence of a "a generalized 12-step consciousness" with "a sociopolitical agenda."[10]

The message was clear: if a majority of the planet's population was codependent or dysfunctional, there was a simple and obvious global solution—12-step therapy for everyone! Thus literally hundreds of 12-step groups have appeared purporting to deal with almost every behavioral "disease" or "addiction" imaginable.

In his 1989 book, *Diseasing of America*, author-psychologist Stanton Peele questions the efficacy of these new 12-step programs and describes the recovery movement as being "out of control." He includes an important quote by Donald Goodwin:

> Therapists "invented" the concept that adult children of alcoholics have special problems that can be treated through therapy. They were able to sell this concept to the public and now they are eligible for reimbursement from insurance companies. In short, . . . it was a way for therapists to tap into a new market and make money.[11]

This all came to a head in the fall of 1991. At the national conference of the American Association for Marriage and Family Therapy, author-psychiatrist Steven J. Wolin, a keynote speaker, publicly denounced the ACoA and Codependence movements, stating that: " . . . the recovery movement and its lopsided counsel of damage has become dangerous." After this denunciation he received a standing ovation from the 5000 members in attendance. When a ranking member of the "inner child" (ACoA) movement was asked by a reporter from *USA Today* to reply to this speech, he responded by stating, "They're just jealous of all the money we're making."[12]

The most noteworthy fact about the growth of the 12-step movement is that its growth has been lateral as well as vertical. This is a result of the basic 12-step belief structure and approach to problem behaviors. AA and other 12-step groups are not bastions of scientific research and intellectual inquiry. Twelve-step organizations are, in fact, perhaps best known for the activities in which they do *not* engage. Twelve-step groups do not charge fees, conduct scientific research, sponsor scientific research, make clinical diagnoses, promote medical treatments, keep attendance records, or maintain membership lists. Their "spiritual" approach is the antithesis of the scientific method. They have The Truth as far as the treatment of addictions goes, and their primary task is to "carry [their 12-step] message" to others. And that message is the same for everyone.

As new 12-step groups have formed, they've applied the same one-size-fits-all philosophy of AA to new areas of perceived dysfunction. This has been done in the near-total absence of scientific (research) support for this approach, and with total disregard for well-supported but non-12-step therapies for some of these behaviors. Within the 12-step movement, any self-defeating or compulsive behavior is met with the same prescription: application of AA's 12 steps with changes of single terms in the first and twelfth steps.

Probably no one knows how many 12-step organizations there are in this country, but the following list gives a hint at their breadth: Adult Children of Alcoholics; Alcoholics Victorious; Al-Anon; Alateen; A.R.T.S. Anonymous (Artists Recovering through the Twelve Steps); Cocaine Anonymous; Codependents Anonymous; C.O.S.A. (Codependents of Sex Addicts); Debtors Anonymous; Dual Disorders Anonymous; Emotional Health Anonymous; Emotions Anonymous; Ethics Anonymous; Families Anonymous; Gamblers Anonymous; Incest Survivors Anonymous; Narcotics Anonymous; Nicotine Anonymous; Obsessive Compulsive Anonymous; Overeaters Anonymous; Pill Addicts Anonymous; Pills Anonymous; Prostitutes Anonymous; Sex Addicts Anonymous; Sex and Love Addicts Anonymous; Sexaholics Anonymous; Unwed Parents Anonymous; and Workaholics Anonymous. In recent months, there have even been Internet reports of Clutterers Anonymous. This might be a joke, but then again it might not.

An extreme example of the tendency to apply 12-step ideology to almost any human problem can be found in the September-October 1994 issue of the *National Association for Children of Alcoholics Newsletter*. In it, Stephanie Abbot, M.A., reviews a book entitled *Vessels of Rage, Engines of Power: The Secret History of Alcoholism*, by James Graham. In her review, Abbot states:

> With the alcoholic's special need for power some of them become murderous. He [Graham] notes that serial killers have egomania: a strong desire to control and humiliate. For many, such as John Gacy and Ted Bundy, that egomania was caused by alcoholism. Recovery from alcoholism with "ego deflation in depth" would have made the murders psychologically impossible.[13]

Graham also attributes the behavior of prominent historical figures such as Joseph Stalin to alcoholism. He writes:

> Theories abound for the cause of Stalin's ruthless and, most often, senseless killings, but to my knowledge no one has yet advanced the idea that alcoholism was the root cause. But I am convinced that anyone knowledge-able about alcoholism who studies his biographies as I have will agree with my conclusion: Stalin was an alcoholic and it was his alcoholism-induced megalomania that drove him to murder millions.[14]

In his book *Diseasing of America*, Stanton Peele describes the logical conclusion to the formulaic 12-step movement:

A 1987 tract, *When Society Becomes an Addict*, claimed that we live in an addictive world, that our entire society is predicated on addiction and denial, and that therefore we need to implement a massive 12-step program for *everyone*, making the government a kind of extension of AA.[15]

As for the size of the larger 12-step movement, it's almost impossible to accurately gauge. But one indication is that the size of Narcotics Anonymous (NA), by far the largest of the other 12-step groups, was approximately 375,000 in 1998.[16] Although there are probably hundreds of other 12-step groups, most are small. As well, interest in the broader 12-step movement (especially ACoA and codependence) seems to have all but vanished (at least in the media) in recent years, and it's reasonable to surmise that it, like AA, peaked in the late 1980s and early 1990s. The broader 12-step movement (with the notable exceptions of Narcotics Anonymous, Marijuana Anonymous, and Cocaine Anonymous), however, does not have access to AA's primary source of new members: individuals coerced into attendance. Given this, and the very noticeable decline in interest in 12-step groups in recent years, it's reasonable to surmise that membership in the broader 12-step movement dropped significantly in the mid and late 1990s. So, a reasonable estimate of total 12-step group membership in the U.S. at the turn of the new millennium (including AA) is in the range of two to three million individuals, with the lower figure probably being closer to the actual figure.

12-Step Groups and Meetings

Twelve-step meetings are held in a variety of locations—churches, schools, libraries, rented meeting halls, and many other places. Addiction treatment centers often provide space at no cost, given that many (almost certainly most) of them believe that "real recovery" takes place in AA (or NA). In addition, AA members often band together to form clubs (e.g., Alano clubs) and establish clubhouses which are used exclusively for 12-step meetings and socialization among 12-steppers.

Like their locations, the size of 12-step meetings varies greatly. They can consist of as few as two or three members, or they can range up to several hundred attendees at "speaker meetings" at which established group members present their stories to an audience. In keeping with AA traditions, all members remain anonymous at meetings, and everyone is addressed and refers to him or herself by first name only (but many members do know each others' true identities—they just don't use last names at meetings or, often, in conversation). The demographic nature of meetings also varies greatly. In most cases, meetings are free and open to anyone. However, in many wealthy neighborhoods meetings are held in private homes by invitation only. As well, about two-thirds of AA members are male. And in many AA and NA meetings, a great number of those attending (often a majority) are individuals not there of their own free will; in other words, a great many of those attending are there under court order, as a condition of probation or parole, or as a condition of maintaining employment or professional certification.

Twelve-step meetings tend to be highly ritualized, and the format and sequence of events is very familiar to group members. First, members will identify themselves in ritualized fashion with their "disease." ("Hi, I'm Jim. I'm an alcoholic.") There will then often be a reading from AA's "inspired" text, the Big Book (often its 12 steps), followed by a sermon by an experienced member (a confession of downfall due to drinking followed by redemption by AA and the speaker's "HP"—Higher Power), "sharing," the taking of a collection, and a final prayer (usually the Lord's Prayer).

New members are told that alcoholism is a disease that is never completely cured, and that they must attend AA for life, the only alternatives being "jails, institutions, or death." They are initially led to believe that their "Higher Power" can be anything they choose, though the wording of the 12 steps makes it clear that this "Higher Power" is a patriarchal deity. This deception is routinely employed, and its purpose is to ease the new member into the conversion process. The results of this conversion process are described by Bill Wilson in the book *Alcoholics Anonymous Comes of Age*: "Nearly every A.A. [member] has a spiritual experience that quite transforms his outlook and attitudes. Ordinarily, such occurrences are gradual and may take place over periods of months or even years."[17]

In *Twelve Steps and Twelve Traditions*, Wilson is much more specific about the nature of this "transform[ation]":

So, practicing these Steps, we had a spiritual awakening about which finally there was no question. Looking at those who were only beginning and still doubted themselves, the rest of us were able to see the change setting in. From great numbers of such experiences, we could predict that the doubter who still claimed that he hadn't got the "spiritual angle," and who still considered his well-loved A.A. group the higher power, would presently love God and call Him by name.[18]

Twelve step members are told that they must accept the "program" as a "way of life," and are expected to abandon their old belief system and conform to the beliefs of the "collective group consciousness." (They are also expected to abandon all former drinking friends and any other friends and family members who are critical of 12-step programs.) In reference to this practice, addictions professional Nancy R. Rader writes:

> I once made the mistake of suggesting . . . that one doesn't need to declare oneself powerless . . . and the A.A. member who I shared this with recoiled in horror. I agree . . . that it isn't wise to attack believers for the belief. But who *does* question the faith of members? A.A. does! And one priest in A.A. told me that the accepted practice of advising newcomers that their "higher power" could be anything could be justified as a means of bringing the addict to see the "truth" in easy stages.[19]

The nature of 12-step groups is well described in the pamphlet entitled *Al-Anon Spoken Here*, in which operational guidelines for the running of meetings are outlined.[20] In Al-Anon meetings, only Al-Anon "conference approved" literature can be read and discussed. Therapy, therapists, and professional terminology are taboo topics. Other recovery or treatment programs are not to be mentioned, and sources of information from outside the "program" are considered objectionable, because they "dilute" the spiritual nature of the meetings. Such limitations on discussion and freedom of inquiry are prevalent throughout the wider 12-step movement.

In addition, 12-step programs offer their membership what is, in essence, the antithesis of therapy. Within AA and Al-Anon, for example, there is no cure; one is always "recovering" but never recovers. The solution provided by these programs is the embrace of "spirituality" and protracted, endless attendance at meetings. An old program slogan puts it best: "You never graduate from Al-Anon."

If an individual 12-step group member isn't "getting it," isn't making what is considered adequate progress, the typical view is that he or she isn't "working the program" properly. The usual prescription is for such a person to attend more meetings. In other words, the view is that the program is perfect and that any problems individual members have in working it are invariably their own fault. This is a form of group denial: that the program can never be the problem or even part of the problem.

One indication of the inbred, dogmatic, we-have-the-answer nature of AA, Al-Anon, and other 12-step programs is that from the start they have not only restricted reading material to their own conference-approved materials, but that they have published their own materials. In hindsight, instituting this practice was a very shrewd move on Bill Wilson's part. The first benefit to AA was that it could sell its literature directly to its members and institutions at discounted prices, yet still realize larger profit margins than could be obtained through commercial distribution and royalties from an outside publishing house. The second benefit entailed control: Alcoholics Anonymous has maintained absolute control over the nature and content of all literature used in AA meetings. A third benefit to Wilson was that he had to put up no personal funds whatsoever, yet he could expect to receive standard hardcover royalties (much higher than paperback royalties) for the rest of his life. As we saw earlier, he and his heirs received millions of dollars in such royalties.

AA's Similarities to Religious Cults

In 1965, author-psychologist Arthur H. Cain had an article in the *Saturday Evening Post* in which he charged AA with being a "dogmatic cult." He wrote:

> Behind the A.A. fence the original principle that alcoholics must be humble before God has been turned into the dictum that alcoholics are God's chosen people. This theme is preached in meetings and through books and pamphlets.[21]

One still commonly hears such talk from AA members, including at times the self-descriptive phrase "better than well" or similar self-congratulatory terms.

Author Charles Bufe, in his book, *Alcoholics Anonymous: Cult or Cure? (second edition)*, addresses the issue at considerably more length than Cain. He lists 23 criteria for determining whether or not an organization is a cult, and compares AA's characteristics with those criteria. He also makes a distinction between "communal AA" (the familiar community meetings) and "institutional AA" (the 12-step treatment industry, which Bufe considers an extension of AA, not an independent entity). Bufe asks:

1. Is Alcoholics Anonymous religiously oriented? Unequivocally yes.

He cites AA's origins in the evangelical Protestant Oxford Group Movement, its religious terminology in the 12 steps and Big Book, and its practice of group prayer as evidence.

2. Is AA irrational, does it discourage skepticism and rational thinking? Again, yes.

As evidence he cites AA's emphasis on "overcoming" doubts and its use of slogans such as "Utilize, don't analyze" and "Your best thinking got you here."

3. Is AA dogmatic? Unfortunately, yes.

He notes the reverence many AA members have toward the Big Book; the often extreme hostility which meets any criticism of its "received wisdom"; and the insistence that the AA program is perfect, and that any fault always lies with those who don't properly "work it."

4. Do AA members have a "chosen people" mentality. Yes.

Bufe cites the "dry drunk" putdown of abstinent former drunks who reject AA, and the self-congratulatory "better than well" terminology often used by AA members.

5. Does AA elevate its own ideology over experience, observation and logic? Again, unequivocally yes.

As evidence, Bufe mentions that AA "ignores the mountains of [scientific] evidence that AA is quite probably ineffective . . . [and] may actually do more harm than good . . . while hypocritically presenting AA as the only road to recovery."

6. Is AA separatist? Yes, but only somewhat more so than other special interest groups.

Here Bufe mentions AA's use of jargon and specialized meanings for standard terms (such as "sobriety"), but he does not mention perhaps the strongest evidence of AA's separatism: that AA members are expected to drop not only their drinking friends, but also any friends and family members who are critical of "the program."

7. Does AA see itself as the exclusive holder of the truth? Unfortunately, yes—at least in regard to the treatment of alcohol abuse.

To support this conclusion, Bufe cites AA's utter disregard of scientific evidence of its inefficacy, as well as the routine assertion by AA members that AA is the *only* way to deal with an alcohol problem.

8. Does AA claim to have special knowledge that will only be revealed to the initiated? A qualified no.

Bufe states that AA has no special knowledge that will be revealed only to the initiated, but it "does claim that 'working a good program' or 'working the steps' leads to 'serenity' and (at least often) 'a spiritual awakening.'"

9. Does AA employ mind-control techniques? For the most part, in communal AA, no. In institutional AA, yes.

Bufe notes that "In institutional AA . . . coerced participants are kept very busy, given little time alone, deprived of outside contacts, allowed to read only approved (that is, indoctrination) literature, forced into making false confessions, subjected to attacks, threats, and ridicule for raising questions or making critical comments, and subjected to extreme pressure by a unanimous majority to change their belief systems."

10. Does AA employ thought-stopping language? Yes, but its employment is less stringent than in many religious cults.

To support this, Bufe states that AA widely employs slogans such as "Keep It Simple, Stupid (KISS)," "Your best thinking got you here," and "Utilize, don't analyze" "to short circuit critical thinking."

11. Does AA manipulate its members through guilt? Yes.

Here, Bufe mentions the moralistic terms in AA's steps and literature, such as the fourth step's "moral inventory," and the intense guilt that AA members feel after "slipping"—guilt which is played upon to tie them closer to AA.

12. Does AA employ "the cult of confession"? Does it use confession for purification and to tie its members to it? Yes.

Bufe notes that AA employs four distinct types of confession: "1) private confession from 'pigeon' to sponsor . . . ; 2) public confession by speakers at AA meetings; 3) public confession by participants at AA meetings; and 4) in institutional AA, false confession."

13. Does AA have a charismatic leader? No, although it does have dead saints.

Even though there is widespread veneration of AA's cofounders within the organization, Bufe states that AA's decentralized, democratic structure ensures that no charismatic leader exists within AA and that none could arise.

14. Does AA have an authoritarian, hierarchical structure? As for communal AA, definitely no. As for institutional AA, yes.

According to Bufe, "communal AA is a model of anarchist organization," but institutional AA is comprised of "corporations or government agencies, which, of course, are hierarchically organized and authoritarian."

15. Does AA insist on submission of the individual to the "will of God?" As for communal AA, yes and no. As for institutional AA, yes.

Here, Bufe points to AA's third step, which instructs members to turn their lives and wills over to God. However, he also points out "that there is no charismatic leader, authoritarian hierarchy, or priest caste in AA to act as interpreter(s) of 'God's will'"; but he then goes on, "in institutional AA, the paid staff often take on this role."

16. Is AA self-absorbed? Absolutely.

Bufe cites several pieces of evidence to show this, such as AA's utter lack of concern for scientific research, the fact that its literature deals only with itself, the near-continual trumpeting of AA as the only way to deal with alcohol problems, and the hostility exhibited by many AA members and AA front groups toward non-12-step recovery programs.

17. Does AA have dual purposes? As for both communal and institutional AA, yes.

To substantiate this, Bufe points out that while AA members tout AA as the answer to alcoholism, AA is at heart a religious indoctrination program. To bolster this point, he refers to AA's self-absorption and its refusal to refer individuals to other recovery programs, and he reminds us that "AA's sole purpose is to 'carry this [religious] message.'" He neglects, however, to point out that the heart of AA's program, the 12 steps, mentions alcohol in only two steps, while it mentions God or synonyms for it (Him, His, Power greater than ourselves) in fully six, and that it specifically advises prayer. This is perhaps the best evidence of AA's dual purposes (posing as an alcohol abuse self-help group, when it is in fact a religious indoctrination program).

18. Does Alcoholics Anonymous economically exploit its members? As for communal AA, no. As for institutional AA, yes.

Here, Bufe points to the free-of-charge nature of community AA meetings, and to the often extremely high fees charged by institutional AA (the 12-step treatment industry) to its often-coerced clients and their insurers.

19. Does AA employ deceptive recruiting techniques. Yes, arguably.

Bufe notes that "it could be argued that AA (or at least many of its members) does engage in deceptive recruiting by falsely representing AA as the only effective treatment for alcoholism. . . . It should be emphasized, though, that most if not all of those who present this misinformation believe what they say. . . ."

20. Is AA possessive? Does it go to lengths to retain members? No, absolutely not.

Bufe's reasoning here is that because AA members in community meetings normally go no further than making a few friendly phone calls to dropouts, that AA is not possessive. The matter, however, is not quite so open and shut. Because AA deliberately encourages new members to cut ties with drinking friends as well as with any other friends or family members critical of AA, it tends to make new members socially/psychologically dependent upon their new AA "family," which oftentimes makes it extremely difficult for them to leave AA. As well, institutional AA, for financial reasons (so that their insurers will continue to pay), routinely exerts extreme pressure upon coerced clients to stay in treatment until their insurance coverage runs out (at which time they are discharged).

So, a more accurate answer to these questions would be: "For communal AA, a qualified no. For institutional AA, yes."

21. Does AA provide a closed, all-encompassing environment? As for communal AA, no. As for institutional AA, yes.

As Bufe points out, even making the commonly prescribed 90 meetings in 90 days in communal AA is hardly "a closed, all-encompassing environment." But as for institutional AA, a great many—in fact a majority—of its clients are coerced into attendance. Once in the confines of institutional AA, their contacts with outside individuals are severely restricted or prohibited altogether, their reading matter is restricted to approved materials, their activities are almost entirely dictated by staff, and they are subjected to often extreme pressure to change their basic beliefs. In fact, the entire purpose of the closed, all-encompassing environment of institutional AA is "ideological indoctrination."

22. Is AA millenarian? In short, no.

The answer to this question is so obvious that Bufe devotes only a single short sentence to it.

23. Does AA employ violence, coercion, and harassment? As for communal AA, no. As for institutional AA, yes—at least as regards coercion.

Bufe states that in regard to communal AA, "the relatively few incidents of harassment directed against groups . . . which are often perceived as rivals to AA, have been mild." But matters in institutional AA are far different: "In many cases, [coerced clients'] alternative to submitting to institutional AA is job loss, imprisonment, suspension or expulsion . . . or decertification (in the case of medical personnel). . . . This gives their warders (the paid staff) tremendous leverage over them, and the warders usually take full advantage of that leverage; they customarily exert a great deal of pressure on such unwilling patients, the purpose of which is to break their resistance to AA."

In conclusion, Bufe compares the number of characteristics of AA that match those of groups commonly described as religious cults, such as Synanon and the People's Temple. He notes that communal AA matches 11 of the above criteria, while institutional AA matches 16. (It should actually be 17, considering the 20th criterion.) In contrast, the Moonies (Unification Church) match 22 of the 23 criteria; the Church of Scientology and the People's Temple match 21 of the criteria; and Synanon matches 20 of them. This leads Bufe to conclude that "AA definitely isn't in the same league with vicious, destructive cults such as the Moonies and the People's Temple, but it does display an alarmingly high number of similarities to such groups. All in all, communal/institutional AA merits the description given to it by Stanton Peele: 'Cult Lite.'"[22]

In his book, *The Real AA*, author Ken Ragge describes the manner in which 12-step groups induce members into conformity of thought. Addictions counselors and AA members customarily suggest that new clients/potential AA members attend 90 meetings in 90 days.
Ragge writes:

In AA, the commitment to 90 meetings in 90 days can greatly limit non-AA social contacts. During this 90-day period of restricted social contact with "normies," every effort is made to discredit non-AA sources of information. The groupers become the sole credible information source for the new member about himself

Imagine, for example, a man who works a 40-hour week and whose daytime hours are spent on the job. After work he heads for a meeting. The meeting lasts for one or two hours. He is then invited to coffee. He has the option of turning down the offer of Fellowship, and may want to since he hasn't seen his family all day. But, in thinking of his family, he may remember a speaker telling of how he almost lost his family [by] not taking advantage of the Fellowship or how another speaker lost his family because he didn't put the program first. In any case, the groupers are friendly and welcoming, and he may have questions. Rather than spending time at home, the newcomer may be off for another hour or two, perhaps longer, receiving what can be considered informal indoctrination.

The groupers do not see themselves as having an ulterior motive. They sincerely want to help and will do their best to do so in the same ways they were helped when they were new.[23]

In this manner newcomers are introduced to the program as a "way of life," and induced to believe that their lives and well-being depend upon "the program." This amounts to a reframing of reality. Stanton Peele describes the negative consequences of this reframing:

1. The conversion experience colors the addict's vision so completely that he or she can offer only the standard line promoted by his or her therapy group.

2. The converted addict loses track of the meanings and motivations in his life, including the significance of his drinking or drug taking and other misbehavior.

3. The new limitations in the person's life—including continued unhealthy behavior such as heavily addicted smoking and coffee drinking and other compulsions, association only with other former addicts and alcoholics, and other ideological blinders—may at times be as problematic as the former addiction.

4. The person is now convinced that single slip will mean a complete return to the addiction or the alcoholism—a fate that befalls many "successful" graduates.

5. All the pitfalls are especially problematic for young people who are convinced that their addictions or other limitations are lifelong and thus learn to define themselves by their problems—problems they more often than not otherwise outgrow.

6. Ex-addicts and recovering alcoholics as therapists are incapable of accepting clients or scientific data that disagree with the tenets of their own therapy.

7. Our society, searching for role models and teachers, increasingly turns for leadership to those least in control and aware of themselves.[24]

Peele could have added other negative consequences of the "diseasing of America," such as that when former addicts and alcoholics return to drinking or drugging after 12-step participation, their problems are often worse, sometimes much worse, than before being exposed to 12-step groups. This is presumably because they believe AA's "one drink, one drunk" and "powerless" dogmas and don't even attempt to control their addictions after 12-step exposure. Still another negative consequence is that millions of individuals waste hour upon hour, year after year in dreary meetings, when they could be getting on with their lives and engaging in constructive activities.

While AA as a whole can be described as either "cult like" or "Cult Lite," depending upon one's preference, one AA spinoff group did become a full-blown religious cult.

Synanon—The Cult that Grew Out of AA

Charles E. Dederich joined Alcoholics Anonymous in California in 1956 and soon became very active in AA, traveling throughout the state to speak at meetings. Within a short time he formed his own group within AA, called the "Tender Loving Care Club." In a controversial move, Dederich invited heroin addicts into his group, which produced a power struggle between the original alcoholic members and the addicts. In 1958 in Santa Monica, his group broke away from AA and founded the nonprofit, tax-exempt corporation, Synanon.[25]

The structure of this new organization was quite different from that of AA, taking the form of a live-in commune. During the 1960s, Dederich's group grew and prospered, deriving much operating income through the sale of corporate promotional items such as ballpoint pens, coffee mugs, desk clocks, tote bags, and other items customized with corporate logos. A large measure of sales success came as the result of the pitch that buying Synanon products generated money for drug rehabilitation.[26]

During its first phase, Synanon I, Synanon functioned as a live-in rehabilitation facility for addicts and alcoholics. Central to its process was a form of attack "therapy" called "The Game," which was a devastating exercise in group cruelty. In the process, individuals were singled out for verbal attacks, which sometimes went on for hours, by the rest of the participating "therapy" group. (Interestingly, although this type of "therapy" has been shown repeatedly in clinical studies to be ineffective, variations of it continue to be used widely in 12-step treatment facilities.)

Despite this abusive form of "therapy," Synanon grew rapidly during the 1960s. Communal living and encounter groups were becoming very popular, and Synanon incorporated both these elements. Eventually,

Synanon began attracting non-alcoholics/addicts, and Dederich decided to create a Synanon II Research and Development Center in order to experiment with alternative lifestyles.[27]

By 1972, Synanon II had attracted 1700 members. Most of these individuals kept their outside jobs, but lived in Synanon housing, ate in communal Synanon dining rooms, and sent their children to Synanon schools. In addition, these new members were required to give most or all of their incomes to the organization. One major difference between Synanon I and Synanon II was that most of the new recruits for Synanon II were neither alcoholics nor addicts; they were "lifestylers." In addition to the shift in membership, there was also a major shift in focus at Synanon: Synanon I's focus had been on rehabilitating addicts and alcoholics; Synanon II's focus was on changing society as a whole.

This new focus spurred resistance from the ex-addicts, who felt betrayed. Although these ex-addicts had been told during the Synanon I phase that they could "graduate," most did not. In his book, *Paradise Incorporated*, former Synanon member David Gerstel explains why:

> Actually, very few addicts did choose to graduate—only 26 in Synanon's first five years of existence. The others who were eligible chose to remain in Synanon. They felt that they would not be able to survive outside the community.[28]

Dederich moved to break any internal resistance to the new and presumably improved Synanon. In a modified and expanded form of The Game, which he called "Perpetual Stew," Dederich forced the ex-addicts to conform or leave. This new version of The Game was "perpetual," because it ran nonstop in shifts, with members taking successive turns.

Dederich's utopian plans did not work out as he expected them to: membership dropped to 1000 by the late 1970s. This drop in membership was largely a result of Dederich's turning Synanon into a religious/corporate cult with Dederich as its guru in the mid 1970s.

The first pronounced change involved militarization. Dederich created what was called the "Punk Squad," which served not only as a reform program for the most difficult Synanon children, but acted as an obedience-enforcing program for all Synanon children. He also initiated a boot camp in which new recruits as well as existing members were required to learn military tactics, presumably in part to instill discipline in them.

Other requirements were imposed on Synanon's members. In 1975, both male and female members were forced to shave off their hair. In 1977, all men who had belonged to Synanon for at least five years—with the single exception of Charles Dederich—were forced to have vasectomies, and all pregnant women were forced to have abortions. And in that same year all Synanon members were assigned new sex partners. In 1978, Dederich declared Synanon a religion.

Synanon eventually collapsed after its goon squad attempted in 1978 to assassinate attorney Paul Morantz, who was representing disaffected members, by placing a rattlesnake in his mailbox. Morantz was bitten on his left hand and nearly died. Dederich and two other Synanon members (one being Lance Kenton, band leader Stan Kenton's son) pleaded no contest to attempted murder. AA alumnus and Synanon founder Charles Dederich was apparently so drunk on the day of his arrest, December 2, 1978, that he was unable to understand the proceedings at his arraignment, and the presiding judge postponed the arraignment until the following day. While Synanon shriveled following the attempted assassination of Morantz, it survives to this day—as a small community/law school in the Sierra Nevada foothills.

During the 1950s and 1960s, Synanon was viewed as a miracle rehabilitation organization and (like the organization from which it had sprung, AA) it received a great deal of favorable press. It wasn't until the bizarre events of the mid and late 1970s—such as the forced vasectomies and abortions—that critical pieces began to appear in the media. Had Dederich not become so viciously irrational in the end, Synanon would probably have survived and prospered as a "rehabilitation" program. Even today, some of its techniques—especially modified forms of The Game— are still widely used in 12-step treatment facilities. And some of those using such techniques acknowledge their source without a hint of embarrassment.

---

1. *Alcoholics Anonymous Comes of Age*, by Bill Wilson. New York: Alcoholics Anonymous World Services, 1957, pp. 74–76.
2. Ibid., p. 180.
3. *Dr. Bob and the Good.Oldtimers*, no author listed. New York: Alcoholics Anonymous World Services, 1980, p. 55.
4. *Pass It On*, no author listed. New York: Alcoholics Anonymous World Services, 1984, pp. 207–210.
5. Ibid., p. 190–192.
6. http://www.alcoholics-anonymous.org/english/E_FactFile/M-24_d4.html
7. *Adult Children of Alcoholics*, by Janet Gerringer Woititz. Hollywood, FL: Health Communications, 1983.
8. *Co-Dependence Mistreated-Misunderstood*, by Anne Wilson Schaef. San Francisco: Harper & Row, 1986, pp. 18–19.
9. *Recovery: A Guide for Adult Children of Alcoholics*, by Herbert Gravitz and Julie D. Bowden. New York: Simon and Schuster, 1987.

10. "Healing Ourselves and Our Planet," by Robin Room. *Contemporary Drug Problems*, Volume 9, Winter 1992, pp. 717–740.

11. *Diseasing of America*, by Stanton Peele. Lexington, MA: Lexington Books, 1989, p. 115.

12. "The Challenge Model: Discovering Resiliency in Children at Risk," by Steven J. Wolin and Sybil Wolin. *The Brown University Child and Adolescent Behavior Letter*, Volume 9, March 1993, p. 1.

13. "The Secret History" (book review), by Stephanie Abbot. *The National Association for Children of Alcoholics Network*, Volume 10, Sept./Oct. 1994, p. 3.

14. *Vessels of Rage, Engines of Power*, by James Graham. Lexington, VA: Aculeus, Press, 1994, p. 170.

15. Peele, op. cit., p. 231.

16. *Narcotics Anonymous: A Commitment to Community Partnerships* [on-line], 1998. Http://www.wsoinc.com/sandiego.htm. For an analysis of this document see *Resisting 12-Step Coercion: How to Fight Forced Participation in AA, NA, or 12-Step Treatment*, by Stanton Peele, Charles Bufe, and Archie Brodsky. Tucson, AZ: See Sharp Press, 2000, p. 22.

17. Wilson, op. cit., p. 63.

18. *Twelve Steps and Twelve Traditions*, by Bill Wilson. New York: Alcoholics Anonymous World Services, 1953, p. 109.

19. "The Last Word," by Nancy W. Rader. *The Humanist*, September/October 1997, p. 2.

20. *Al-Anon Spoken Here*, no author listed. New York: Al-Anon Family Group Headquarters, 1984.

21. "Alcoholics Anonymous: Cult or Cure?" by Arthur Cain. *Saturday Evening Post*, September 19, 1965.

22. *Alcoholics Anonymous: Cult or Cure? (Second Edition)*, by Charles Bufe. Tucson, AZ: See Sharp Press, 1998, pp. 143–157.

23. *The Real AA: Behind the Myth of 12-Step Recovery*, by Ken Ragge. Tucson, AZ: See Sharp Press, 1998, p. 105.

24. Peele, op. cit., p. 112.

25. *Paradise Incorporated*, by David U. Gerstel. Novato, CA: Presidio Press, 1982, p. 36.

26. "Selling Synanon," by Mark Clifford. *Forbes*, Volume 137 Number 12, June 2, 1986.

27. *The Light on Synanon*, by Dave Mitchell, Cathy Mitchell, and Richard Ofshe. New York: Seaview Books, 1980, p. 151.

28. Gerstel, op. cit., p. 37.

6

The Disease Concept of Alcoholism and Its Outgrowths

Early studies of alcohol consumption centered on the nutritional value of alcohol. Toward the end of the 19th century, the new American industrial management techniques gave rise to research on the effects of alcohol on worker productivity and fatigue; but with the advent of prohibition, alcohol research came to a standstill in America. After the repeal of prohibition, research concerning the nature and effects of alcohol consumption experienced a rebirth. To quote E.M. Jellinek:

> This relatively long period of disinterest sufficed to relegate the efforts of proponents of the illness conception to oblivion, but somehow the idea that "alcoholism" was an illness was lurking to be "rediscovered."[1]

Alcohol studies became important during the 1930s due in part to the sharp rise in the use of motor vehicles for personal as well as commercial-industrial transport; with this came a corresponding increase in alcohol-related traffic accidents. Because of such accidents, law enforcement officials needed accurate tests to determine levels of alcohol intoxication.

In order for such testing to become a reality, research was needed to determine the manner in which the human body metabolized alcohol. So, in 1937, a group of psychiatrists and psychologists founded the Research Council on Problems of Alcohol at Yale University. Through a research grant, the newly established Council funded a study to review the existing body of scientific data available on alcoholism. This grant was awarded to a man named E. M. Jellinek, who would become a pivotal figure within the American recovery movement.

The Father of the Disease Concept

Elvin Morton Jellinek was born in New York City in 1890 and held degrees from the universities of Berlin, Grenoble, and Leipzig. During the 1920s, he was employed in botanical research in Central America; during the 1930s he worked as a biometrician (one who applies scientific statistical data to physiology) at a hospital in Worcester, Massachusetts.[2] Prior to accepting the grant from the Research Council, Jellinek showed little or no interest in alcohol-related studies.

Much of the data reviewed by Jellinek came from the work of the Medical Association for the Study of Inebriety and Narcotics, which had been published in *The Journal of Inebriety*. (See Chapter 1) This is a telling comment on the state of alcohol research in the United States at the time, as *The Journal of Inebriety* had ceased publication in 1914, and the "newest" data in it was nearly a quarter-century old.

In 1940, the Research Council on Problems of Alcohol began publishing a research periodical called the *Quarterly Journal of Studies on Alcohol* (QJSA), later known as the *Journal of Studies on Alcohol* (JSA). Within this journal, the term "inebriety" was replaced by the term "alcoholism," and the cluster of behaviors associated with the term was first described as a "disease."[3] The JSA is still one of the leading journals in the field of alcohol studies.

After completing the initial research grant project, Jellinek was hired by Dr. Howard Haggard, director of the Laboratory of Applied Physiology at Yale, in order to allow him to continue research within the section on alcohol studies. Jellinek's activities within the field were wide ranging. He founded the Yale Center on Alcohol Studies, the Yale Summer School of Alcohol Studies, and the Yale Plan Clinics for the treatment of alcoholism, and he served as a consultant to the Alcoholism Subcommittee of the World Health Organization. In addition, with AA member and PR writer Marty Mann, he co-founded what is now the National Council on Alcoholism and Drug Dependence. In 1960, his book, *The Disease Concept of Alcoholism*, appeared. It outlined his final conclusions which, in large part, became the basis for treatment of alcohol abuse in the United States.

Through Jellinek's work and publications—and its association with Yale University—the Yale Center assumed the aura of scientific credibility. In conjunction with the initial study grant, Yale University created an indexed and fully abstracted library containing research materials and literature concerning addiction. In 1943, the Yale Summer School of Alcohol Studies was organized in order to educate concerned citizens and authorities on the new disease concept. A year later, the first of the Yale Plan clinics opened and treatment based on the disease concept became a reality.

A Common Formulation of the Disease Concept

In her book, *Alcoholism: The Genetic Inheritance*, author Kathleen Whalen Fitzgerald lists the commonly accepted assumptions in the addictions treatment community concerning the Jellinek disease model. Hers is a good summation of disease-concept beliefs:

1. The Jellinek disease victim is suffering from a bona fide disease that is killing him and is destroying his family.
2. Denial is a basic part of his disease; the purpose of the intervention is to pierce his denial so that he will see the reality of his disease and seek treatment.
3. Because Jellinek's disease is chronic and progressive, no goal other than that of total abstinence from alcohol and other mood altering substances is acceptable.
4. Most importantly, all concerned must acknowledge that Jellinek's disease is the primary cause of the alcoholic's condition. Financial, marital, health, and other problems are effects of untreated Jellinek's disease; they have not caused the drinking.
5. Treatment at a specific rehabilitation center is a must. Time has run out for trying it alone.[4]

Fitzgerald also outlines the goals of a successful treatment program:

1. That the person emerges with a commitment to a life of total abstinence from alcohol and other mood altering drugs.
2. That he accepts the fact that he has a chronic, progressive, fatal disease and that he understands the nature of this disease.
3. That some of the damage his drinking has caused him and his family starts to heal.
4. That he begins the long process of personal change that will insure his personal sobriety.[5]

This interpretation of the new disease concept of alcoholism is, however, remarkably similar to the old illness concept of inebriety found within the studies in *The Journal of Inebriety*. In his book, *American Temperance Movements: Cycles of Reform*, Jack S. Blocker writes:

Despite its lack of originality, Jellinek's formulation of the disease concept of alcoholism framed most aspects of modern debate over the nature of alcoholism and its treatment. That it did so is due less to the force of the formulation itself than to Jellinek's work as a publicist, which in turn seems to have profited enormously from the connection Jellinek and his closest associates had with Yale University.[6]

Elaboration of the Disease Concept

The first Jellinek disease model (1941) was the product of his collaborative effort with a psychiatrist named Karl Bowen. It contains 24 typological formulations of "alcoholic" using the phylum method of classification.[7][8] According to author William White, this was condensed down to 14 classifications the following year, and the phylum system was discarded.[9]

The final model outlined in Jellinek's 1960 book, *The Disease Concept of Alcoholism*, contains five "species" or classifications of alcoholism:

1. Alpha alcoholism represents a *purely* psychological *continual* dependence upon the effect of alcohol to relieve bodily or emotional pain. The drinking is "undisciplined" in the sense that it contravenes such rules as society tacitly agrees upon—such as time, occasion, locale, amount and effect of drinking —*but does not lead to "loss of control" or "[in]ability to abstain."* The damage caused by this species of alcoholism may be restricted to the disturbance of interpersonal relations. There may also be interference with the family budget, occasional absenteeism from work and decreased productivity, and some of the nutritional deficiencies of alcoholism, [but] not the disturbances due to withdrawal of alcohol. *Nor are there any signs of a progressive process.*

2. Beta alcoholism is that species of alcoholism in which such alcoholic complications as polyneuropathy, gastritis and cirrhosis of the liver may occur without either physical or psychological dependence upon alcohol. The incentive to heavy drinking that leads to such complications may be the custom of a certain social group in conjunction with poor nutritional habits. The damage in this case is of course the nutritional deficiency diseases, but impaired family budget as well as a curtailed life span may also occur. Withdrawal symptoms, on the other hand, do not emerge.

3. Gamma alcoholism means that species of alcoholism in which (1) acquired increased tissue tolerance to alcohol, (2) adaptive cell metabolism, (3) withdrawal symptoms and "craving" i.e. physical dependence, and (4) loss of control are involved. In gamma alcoholism there is a definite progression from psychological to physical dependence and marked behavior changes such as have been described previously.

This species produces the greatest and most serious kinds of damage. The loss of control, of course, impairs interpersonal relations to the highest degree. The damage to health in general and to financial and social standing are also more prominent than in other species of alcoholism.

4. Delta alcoholism shows the first three characteristics of gamma alcoholism as well as a less marked form of the fourth characteristic—that is, instead of loss of control there is an ability to "go on the water wagon" for even a day or two without the manifestation of withdrawal symptoms; the ability to control the amount of intake on any given occasion, however, remains intact. The incentive to high intake may be found in the general acceptance of the society to which the drinker belongs, while pre-alcoholic psychological vulnerability may be of a low degree.

5. Epsilon alcoholism among these other species is periodic alcoholism, which in Europe and Latin America is still designated as dipsomania, a term in disuse in North America. We may denote it as Epsilon alcoholism, but it will be neither described or defined here, as it seems to be the least known species of alcoholism. In the course of their periodic bouts, epsilon alcoholics may cause serious damage.

In describing these species of alcoholism, Jellinek writes:

> In spite of the respect and admiration to which Alcoholics Anonymous have a claim on account of their great achievements, there is every reason why the student of alcoholism should emancipate himself from accepting the picture of alcoholism as propounded by Alcoholics Anonymous. Alcoholics Anonymous have naturally created the picture of alcoholism in their own image. . . .[10]

Ironically, as we'll see below, Jellinek's view of alcoholism was itself largely a product of AA.

Within AA there's a popular slogan: "Take what you want and leave the rest." This is apparently what happened with Jellinek's disease concept of alcoholism. Jellinek's disease concept or model did not conform entirely to the philosophy and principles of AA, so only the most severe type, the gamma species, was incorporated as the basis of practice within the American addictions treatment community. The bulk of the disease concept/model was ignored and discarded. Only the gamma model and the conclusions flowing from it (as enumerated by Fitzgerald—see p. 85) were and are acceptable to AA and the U.S. treatment system. From the very beginning, AA and the 12 steps (a program initially intended only for severe alcoholics) have dominated the treatment community and the recovery movement. And they continue to do so.

Development of the Disease Concept

The disease concept of addiction as currently known in the U.S. can be traced back to one survey which was conducted by Jellinek in collaboration with AA in its early days in 1945, and which was distributed through the

AA organ, *The Grapevine*. AA was relatively small at the time, so the response to the survey was also small; only 158 of the questionnaires were filled out and returned out of a total of approximately 1,600 circulated. Of the 158 questionnaires returned, 15 were filled out by female AA members, and these were excluded from analysis because on the one hand the number was too small to be analyzed separately, and on the other hand the answers differed so greatly from those given by men that merging the question-naires would have skewed the results. Seventeen questionnaires were not properly filled out as the subjects did not state their ages in relation to the questions, but simply answered "yes" or "no." And 28 members of one AA group pooled their information and recorded their averages only. So, the total number of questionnaires Jellinek analyzed was only 98.[11]

Thus the basis of American addictions treatment as embodied by the 12-step Minnesota Model was in a very real sense derived from this one incomplete, obviously flawed study—which utilized an AA-designed survey of a small sample of self-selected, male AA members, and which didn't even have a non-AA comparison group.

The results of this survey were published in 1946 in the *Quarterly Journal of Studies on Alcohol*. For such shoddy research to appear in a professional journal would be unheard of in more modern times. However, the reason for publication of Jellinek's piece is obvious in hindsight: Jellinek was the managing editor of the *Quarterly Journal of Studies on Alcohol*. At the time it was the only professional journal in the U.S. dealing with addiction.

In 1950, Jellinek formulated an operational disease model for alco-holism on the basis of this one flawed study. This model was presented at the Yale Summer School of Alcohol Studies in that same year, after which it was submitted to the Alcoholism Subcommittee of the World Health Organization and published in the QJSA in 1952.[12] In this article, Jellinek refers to only one research source: the 1945 *Grapevine* survey of AA members. In this article, "Phases of Alcohol Addiction," Jellinek did not refer to different "species" of alcoholism. He had not yet formulated the complete model. As a result, the disease concept based upon what would eventually be defined as "gamma alcoholism" had a dominating influence upon early treatment. In addition, the monopoly position of AA and its symbiotic relationship with the treatment community assured acceptance of this simplified model (which was very similar to the AA concept of alcoholism).

In 1952, Mark Keller, assistant editor of the QJSA and a consultant to the Alcoholism Subcommittee of the World Health Organization, published an article titled "The Definition of Alcoholism and the Estimation of its Prevalence." In it, Keller writes:

Alcoholism is a psychogenic dependence on or a physiological addiction to ethanol, manifested by the inability of the alcoholic consistently to control either the start of drinking or its termination once started. . . . [It makes] "loss of control" over drinking the pathognomic symptom, in agreement with Jellinek. The significance of loss of control is that it denotes helpless dependence or addiction, the essence of the disease.[13]

In addition, Keller confirmed that the phenomenon of alcoholism (gamma species) is a cross-cultural phenomenon. That is to say, this definition is applicable to anyone who has a drinking problem, and since it is cross cultural, it can apply to anyone on the planet.[14] In this article, Keller cites only two reference sources for the "loss of control" component of the "disease": Jellinek's 1946 and 1952 QJSA articles, which in turn were based on the 1945 *Grapevine* study.

After a 1952 revised reprint of the 1946 Jellinek article, and the 1952 Keller article defining alcoholism, a British doctor named Max Mier Glatt, utilizing the Jellinek model and the Keller definition of alcoholism, created a model of addiction and recovery in 1954, which he labeled a "Jellinek Chart." However, in addition to the symptoms provided by Jellinek, Glatt then proposed a course of recovery in a series of dozens of progressive steps which he also incorporated into his model.

Glatt propounded the gamma species of alcoholism so well that the World Health Organization and the American addictions treatment community accepted this model without question. This is a fundamental flaw which has become embedded and institutionalized within the American chemical dependency field. The notion that there is only one type of alcoholism, gamma alcoholism, that it is a chronic, progressive, and inevitably fatal disease, and that anyone who has any kind of a drinking problem has this specific type of disease, can be traced directly back to E.M. Jellinek, Mark Keller, Max Mier Glatt—and the 98 questionnaires considered in the 1945 AA/Jellinek survey.

This fundamental flaw within the American chemical dependency field—with essentially the entire edifice resting upon this one exceedingly weak reed—has led to neglect, misdiagnosis, and improper treatment of both addicted and nonaddicted alcohol abusers and problem drinkers.

The Selling of the Disease Concept

In 1944, Jellinek and Marty Mann co-founded the National Committee for Education on Alcoholism (NCEA—later the National Council on Alcoholism, and still later the National Council on Alcoholism and Drug

Dependence). Mann, the daughter of wealthy parents, had embarked upon a successful career as a businesswoman and writer until alcohol abuse interrupted her career. Psychiatric counseling apparently did little to help her in dealing with her alcohol problem, and she eventually found her way into Alcoholics Anonymous.

A short while after joining AA, Mann decided to publicize the AA view of alcoholism. She attended the Yale Summer School, and she arranged to meet with Howard Haggard, director of the Yale Center of Alcohol Studies, and E.M. Jellinek, editor of the *Quarterly Journal of Studies on Alcohol*. Jellinek managed to persuade Haggard to fund a grant to Mann, and in October 1944 she and Jellinek co-founded the NCEA, with Mann as executive director and both Bill Wilson's and Dr. Bob Smith's names appearing on its letterhead as advisors. The message of Mann and the NCEA was clear and simple: 1) alcoholism was a disease and not a moral weakness; 2) a treatment for this disease was possible through the organization known as Alcoholics Anonymous.

The collaboration of Mann, Jellinek, and Wilson produced a powerful, well-oiled machine. Wilson, through AA, provided a pool of clients for the Yale Plan alcoholism treatment clinics. Jellinek, through Yale University, provided an aura of scientific credibility to AA and the disease concept, complete with clinics and an educational program to provide instruction in the new treatment methods. And Mann, through the NCEA—in the guise of a disinterested "educational" organization—presented a positive image of AA and the disease concept of alcoholism to the American public.

Initially, there was no opposition to this collaborative effort, as the collaborators held a virtual monopoly position within the field of addictions treatment. Jellinek had become famous as *the* leading authority on the treatment of addictions. Yale, at that time, was the only institution in the country with a school of addiction studies and a professional journal on addictions. The NCEA was the only national "educational" organization devoted to alcohol abuse and its treatment. And, in addition, AA was the only alcohol self-help recovery organization in the country. This was a powerful combination, one which would determine the nature and scope of addictions treatment in the United States for decades.

As the Yale University School of Alcohol Studies indoctrinated students in Jellinek's disease concept of alcoholism, and as it lauded Alcoholics Anonymous, graduates spread across the country preaching the new gospel: alcoholism was not a moral problem but, rather, a medical/spiritual problem, and alcoholism was a treatable disease. This message spread and took deep root. As AA and the disease concept gained acceptance, a model for the standardized treatment of alcoholics emerged during the 1950s and 1960s.

There was, however, some opposition to the disease concept of alcoholism and its demand for abstinence-only treatment. The controversy over Jellinek's disease concept began in 1949. Marty Mann and the National Council for Education on Alcoholism were disseminating material to the public which characterized the disease concept as a sound and scientifically proven reality. Seldon Bacon, the new director of the Yale Center on Alcohol Studies, became alarmed by this. Many of the ideas that Mann and the NCEA were advocating had no hard research evidence to support them. As a result, Bacon and Yale University ended sponsorship of and affiliation with Mann and the NCEA at the end of 1949.[15]

During that same year, the North American Association of Alcoholism Programs was formed. This new organization wanted to broaden treatment options to include moderate-drinking and abstinence goals rather than abstinence-only goals. But little came of this; serious studies of moderate drinking therapy didn't appear in the U.S. for approximately another quarter century, and the Jellinek/Mann/Wilson juggernaut rolled on.

In 1954, Ruth Fox, MD founded what is now known as the American Society of Addiction Medicine (ASAM). Since its founding, ASAM has campaigned tirelessly for the disease concept of alcoholism, AA, 12-step treatment, and acceptance of "addiction medicine as a specialty recognized by the American Board of Medical Specialties." ASAM's close ties to AA and the 12-step "educational" machine can easily be seen in the fact that it was part of the NCADD for over a decade in the 1970s and 1980s. While ASAM still hasn't succeeded in having "addiction medicine" accepted as a recognized specialty, its efforts and those of its allies paid dividends in the years after its founding.

In 1956, the American Medical Association accepted the disease concept of alcoholism, and the American Hospital Association did so in 1957. In 1961, a grant from the National Institute of Mental Health in conjunction with the U.S. Department of Health, Education and Welfare established the Cooperative Commission on the Study of Alcoholism. And in 1967 the Cooperative Commission published *Alcohol Problems: A Report to the Nation*, in which it recommended the implementation of legislation proposed by President Johnson in October 1966, which called for the establishment of a National Center for Prevention and Control of Alcoholism. Fueled by the positive public relations efforts of Marty Mann and the endorsement of AA and the Minnesota Model of treatment by the by-then National Council on Alcoholism (now the National Council on Alcoholism and Drug Dependence—NCADD), public sentiment favored legislative action.

Impact of the Hughes Act

Finally, the U.S. Congress passed landmark legislation, the Comprehensive Alcohol Abuse and Alcoholism Prevention, Treatment and Rehabilitation Act of 1970. This law is more often referred to as the "Hughes Act," after its sponsor, AA member and U.S. Senator Harold Hughes. Passage of this act won Hughes the NCADD's highest honor, the Gold Key Award.[16] The Act established the National Institute on Alcohol Abuse and Alcoholism, which in turn unleashed a torrent of federal cash aimed at alcohol abuse. Part of this river of cash went to the NCADD. Following passage of the Hughes Act, the NIAAA "logically began contracting with NCADD for assistance," and NCADD's budget quintupled, with 75% of the money coming from the federal government.[17]

But much more of the NIAAA cash went to treatment programs and treatment-related programs. As an example, the number of employee assistance programs (EAPs) rose from at most a few hundred at the time of the Hughes Act's passage to approximately 5000 at the end of the 1970s, a more than ten-fold increase.[18] This increase was fostered by the NIAAA, with the active participation of the NCADD. (EAPs funnel "impaired" employees into 12-step treatment, and, as everywhere else in the American alcoholism treatment industry, they are largely staffed by 12-step group members.)

The number of treatment facilities also skyrocketed following passage of the Hughes Act. In addition to the cash provided by the government, there was also a second spur—major insurers such as Blue Cross, Aetna, and Kemper began to offer coverage for alcoholism treatment. While it's difficult to accurately estimate the number of treatment facilities in past decades, due largely to poor surveying and record keeping, it's reasonable to estimate that the number of treatment facilities in the U.S. at least quadrupled in the 1970–1990 period, with there being in excess of 10,000 treatment facilities in 1990. The numbers apparently increased during the following years, and by the late 1990s there were approximately 15,000 treatment facilities in the U.S. treating approximately 2,000,000 persons per year.[19] The number of treated persons appears to have been stable throughout the 1990s.

The Shift to Outpatient Treatment

The apparent increase in the number of treatment facilities during the 1990s runs contrary to popular perception, which is that the treatment industry fell on hard times during the early '90s. In fact, starting around

1989 or 1990 private insurers—faced with numerous studies showing that inpatient treatment was no more effective than much less expensive outpatient treatment—began to be very reluctant to pay for inpatient treatment. So, during the 1990s, not only were insurers covering far fewer clients for inpatient treatment, but they were paying for far fewer days of treatment per client than during the gravy-train years of the 1980s. This put the screws to the for-profit inpatient treatment facilities, and their numbers plummeted.

The cost factor in the shift from inpatient to outpatient treatment should not be underestimated. At the time the shift began, costs for a 28-day stay in private inpatient facilities routinely exceeded $10,000 and often exceeded $20,000. Worse, recidivism rates were sky high, with repeat clients eating up 50% to 70% of public care treatment costs and 30% to 40% of private care treatment costs.[20] A great many inpatient alcohol-treatment clients really did "keep coming back."

So, beginning around 1990, there was a greatly increasing demand for outpatient treatment, and the number of facilities providing such treatment expanded significantly during the decade. At present, outpatient facilities comprise a good majority of treatment facilities, and they see a good majority of alcoholism clients. One interesting aspect of this shift is that there seems to be a bit more choice in outpatient treatment than inpatient treatment programs. The *National Treatment Center Study Summary Report* indicates that 96% of inpatient treatment centers are 12-step facilities, but only 90% of outpatient treatment centers are 12-step facilities. This is still an overwhelming percentage, and in many areas no "alternative" programs are available. Even in places where non-12-step treatment programs exist, one must often do a fair amount of searching to find one. And if one finds one, one must sometimes wait for months for an opening (especially in the rare publicly funded "alternative" programs).

---

1. *The Disease Concept of Alcoholism*, by E.M. Jellinek. Piscataway, NJ: Alcohol Research Documentation, 1960, p. 7.
2. *American Temperance Movements: Cycles of Reform*, by Jack S. Blocker, Jr. Boston: K.G. Hall & Co., 1989, p. 146.
3. Ibid., p. 147.
4. *Alcoholism: The Genetic Inheritance*, by Kathleen Whalen Fitzgerald. New York: Doubleday, 1988, p. 137.
5. Ibid.
6. Blocker, op. cit., p. 154.
7. "The Classification of Alcoholics," by Thomas F. Babor. *Alcohol Health and Research World*, Spring 1996, pp. 6–14.

8. "Alcohol Addiction and its Treatment," by Karl M. Bowen and Elvin M. Jellinek. *Quarterly Journal of Studies on Alcohol*, Volume 2, 1941, pp. 98–176.
9. *Slaying the Dragon: The History of Addiction Treatment in America*, by William L. White. Bloomington, IL: Chestnut Hill Health Systems/Lighthouse Institute Publications, 1998, p. 214.
10. Jellinek, op. cit., pp. 35–41.
11. "Phases of the Drinking History of Alcoholics: Analysis of a Survey Conducted by the Official Organ of Alcoholics Anonymous," by E.M. Jellinek. *Quarterly Journal of Studies on Alcohol*, Volume 7, 1946, p. 6.
12. "Phases of Alcohol Addiction," by E.M. Jellinek. *Quarterly Journal of Studies on Alcohol*, Volume 13, 1952, pp. 673–684.
13. "The Definition of Alcoholism and the Estimation of its Prevalence, by Mark Keller. In D.J. Pittman and R.C. Snyder, eds., *Society, Culture and Drinking Patterns*. New York: John Wiley and Sons, 1962.
14. *A Dictionary of Words About Alcohol*, by Mark Keller and M. McCormick. Rutgers Center of Alcohol Studies, 1968.
15. Blocker, op. cit., p. 154.
16. "For 50 Years, The Voice of Americans Fighting Alcoholism." http://www.ncadd.org/50yrs.html, p. 4.
17. Ibid., p. 5.
18. Ibid.
19. *The Treatment Episode Data Set (TEDS): 1992–1997 National Admissions to Substance Abuse Treatment.* Rock Springs, Maryland: Substance Abuse and Mental Health Services Administration, 1999, p. 112.
20. "Penny Wise, Pound Foolish? (Relapse Prevention)," by Terence Gorski. *Addiction and Recovery Newsletter*, May-June 1992, p. 24.

7

The Addictions Treatment Industry

Formulation of the Minnesota Model

In 1949, a group of wealthy AA members purchased Hazelden Farm, a parcel of land located next to the Wilmar State Mental Hospital in Center City, Minnesota. The farmhouse was turned into a refuge for alcoholics institutionalized at the State Hospital, and became established as the Hazelden Foundation. During the early 1950s, psychologists Daniel J. Anderson and Dr. Nelson J. Bradley, recently educated at the Yale School of Alcohol Studies, began working with alcoholics in the Hazelden facility in conjunction with Wilmar State Hospital. Bradley and Anderson, utilizing Jellinek's disease concept in conjunction with the basic principles and practices of AA, organized and coordinated teams of physicians, social workers, psychologists, clergymen, and AA members to treat alcoholics.[1] Their program became a prototype. Soon, other hospitals within Minnesota copied their treatment techniques and formulated a standardized treatment program for addiction which became known as the "Minnesota Model" and which was subsequently adopted on a national scale.

One initially controversial principle incorporated into this model was taken directly from AA—that only an alcoholic can effectively help another alcoholic. From the very beginnings of the Minnesota Model, addictions counselors were recruited from the ranks of recovering alcoholics. To quote Hazelden co-founder Daniel Anderson: "At that time people thought we were crazy to hire somebody whose only qualification was that he had been a drunkard."[2]

The Minnesota Model standardized the duration of treatment at 28 days Within this time, patients were provided detoxification and medication to alleviate withdrawal symptoms and possible delirium tremens. They were then provided with individual counseling, exposed to educational lectures and films describing the progressive and ultimately fatal nature of Jellinek's non-curable disease, and were subjected to confrontational group counseling in order to overcome their inevitable "denial." In addition, patients were given 12-step literature and were induced into intense involvement in 12-step groups. Variations of the Minnesota Model range from outpatient treatment, which usually lasts six weeks and is intended for addicts/alcoholics who do not require detoxification or 24-hour monitoring, to long-term inpatient treatment, which can last up to six months or longer.

The Minnesota Model extended the role of the hospital in treatment beyond what it had been in the 1930s and 1940s. In that period, the role of hospitals was strictly to provide help with detoxification. This was the type of help Bill Wilson, AA's cofounder, received repeatedly at Towns Hospital in the early 1930s. But the Minnesota Model added psychological counseling and religious/spiritual reprogramming to the menu. In essence, the purely medical aspects of alcohol abuse were to be treated by expensive, qualified medical personnel; this was to be followed by the less expensive counseling/reprogramming provided by low-paid paraprofessionals (AA members with little if any professional training); and this in turn was to be followed by lifetime participation in AA.

The Minnesota Model of treatment had economic and political appeal for obvious reasons. A new army of expensive psychiatrists or psychologists would not have to be educated and trained in order to deal with the "disease" of alcoholism, as much less expensive (in reality, woefully underpaid) paraprofessionals recruited from the ranks of the "recovering" would provide the counseling. The length of treatment would be limited to 28 days, and the follow-up aftercare as provided by AA and other 12-step groups would not cost taxpayers or insurance companies a dime. All that was left was for the medical community to provide the rationale for this treatment approach. It did so early on.

As we saw in the previous chapter, in 1956 the American Medical Association (AMA) recognized alcoholism as a disease. In this recognition, the AMA recommended that there be hospital treatment for alcoholics. In 1957, the American Hospital Association (AHA) also recognized alcoholism as a disease. This echoed the findings of a 1944 special committee of the AHA which, like the AMA, had recommended hospitalization of alcoholics.

In 1965, the American Psychiatric Association also recognized the need for medical treatment of alcohol abuse. It did, however, reject the term "alcoholism."[3]

By 1970, with the passage of the Hughes Act, the disease concept of addiction and the 12-step approach to the treatment of addictions had become institutionalized in the United States. The treatment of addictions had become big business, and its working model was the Minnesota Model.

The Relationship of AA to the Treatment Industry

At about the time of the passage of the Hughes Act, it began to make sense to consider AA as being made up of separate but related components rather than as a monolithic whole. Vince Fox, in his 1993 book, *Addiction, Change & Choice*, lists the primary components of AA:

Communal AA . . . is the AA we all know, the gatherings in church basements of people helping one another and seeking answers to common problems. They talk and listen, give "leads" (short monologues), and share intimacies. They consume doughnuts by the megaton and drink coffee that makes your teeth itch, and they smoke a lot.

Organizational AA . . . is basically the General Service Office of Alcoholics Anonymous, Inc., which oversees its two totally owned subsidiaries, Alcoholics Anonymous World Services, Inc., and Alcoholics Anonymous Grapevine, Inc. . . . It manages a multitude of tasks such as keeping track of sales, salaries, contributions, payment of royalties and writers' fees, insurance, professional and institutional relations, film development, conferences, and foreign literature assistance.

Institutional AA . . . established treatment centers and hospitals that appropriated the AA program, put a price tag on it, and offered it for sale in institutional settings. Communal and Organizational AA painfully adapted to what they could not (and did not even attempt to) control, but in time both developed a love/hate relationship with the thieves [Institutional AA].
. . . In supreme irony, however, the acquisitive ways of the wayward offspring are now encouraged, and even catered to, by the parent—AA's General Service Office. It continues, always *unofficially*, to "cooperate but not affiliate" with Institutional (commercial) AA.[4]

Fox explains the financial relationship of Communal and Organizational AA to Institutional AA: "AA currently operates on a budget of over $10 million dollars per year, about 75% of which comes from the sale of books and other literature—with over half of those sales being to institutions."[5] In other words, Alcoholics Anonymous has become financially dependent upon the addictions treatment industry, and the addictions treatment industry has become dependent upon AA (which supplies its "program" free of charge as well as the bulk of the industry's counselors) in a symbiotic relationship which certainly seems to violate the spirit of AA's traditions (6, 7, and 8) if not their letter.

Just how close the relationship is between AA and the 12-step treatment industry is well illustrated by a man quoted by Fox who had completed a

28-day treatment program while Fox was writing his book. The man states: "It was the most expensive 28-day AA meeting I ever attended."[6]

Efficacy of the Minnesota Model

The vast majority of addictions treatment centers in the United States utilize the Minnesota Model of addictions treatment or variations on it. Virtually all patients entering these facilities will be exposed to the 12 steps and will be encouraged to participate in 12-step groups for the remainder of their lives. Treatment centers promote the concept that alcoholism/ addiction is a chronic, progressive, and inevitably fatal disease, that treatment is essential to recovery, and that 12-step treatment is the best, most effective means of treatment. Addiction treatment centers in conjunction with AA also promote the idea that once an individual is an alcoholic/addict he or she can never recover but only "arrest" the "disease," and that recovery is a life-long process. Treatment centers also impart the idea that the recovery process (utilizing the 12 steps) will progressively and inevitably provide the alcoholic/addict with renewed physical health and emotional well-being. For example, the Jellinek chart published by Parkside Medical Corporation titled "The Progression and Recovery of the Alcoholic in the Disease of Alcoholism" states that the alcoholic will become enlightened and will attain "higher levels [of well-being] than ever before" due to the recovery process.[7]

Due to the widespread projection of this happy-face image of treatment, the public by and large unthinkingly accepts the efficacy of 12-step treatment and questions the need for alternative treatments. Indeed, this is the aim of 12-step proselytizers. Twelve-step supporters could well argue —though they'd never make the argument so openly—that just because the 12 steps as used in the Minnesota Model have a religious origin and are religious in nature, just because 12-steppism is a one-size-fits-all dogma offered as a panacea for so broad a range of problems that everyone in the world is thought to need a 12-step "program," and just because most of the people who administer 12-step treatment are also among the treated and are themselves "recovering" (but never recover), doesn't necessarily prove that there is anything wrong with 12-step treatment. According to this logic, the 12-step model could be wonderfully effective despite all this.

However, it is not. It suffers from two central flaws: 1) the best scientific evidence (controlled studies) indicates that it lacks efficacy; and 2) what is provided as a cure is almost as bad as the malady. Alcoholics Anonymous is a spiritual-religious response to a social, psychological, and medical failure. It came into being because American society provides the social conditions in which alcohol abuse flourishes, and because of the failure of the psychological and psychiatric communities to provide appropriate and adequate care for those addicted to alcohol.

For decades, expensive and lengthy addictions treatment programs have offered the same basic philosophy and methodology as AA as the core of their treatment. Although many treatment centers tout recovery rates as high as 80%, 90%, and even 95%, these rates reflect very short-term abstinence; one-year follow-up studies are considered "long term." And in calculating these astoundingly high recovery rates, treatment centers typically count neither treatment dropouts nor those with whom they've lost contact.

The figures provided by writers vary drastically. Terence Gorski and G. Alan Marlatt report that during the 1980s Minnesota Model facilities produced one-year recovery rates as high as 65% in as many as one-third of U.S. addictions treatment centers.[8] However, George Vaillant in his *Natural History of Alcoholism* states that the 67% rate of improvement reported in a Rand Corporation study proved to be an "illusion" produced through design flaws, "ignoring the law of initial values," and by not including "attrition."[9] In a separate article, Gorski concedes that there is an overall 75% relapse rate among those who have undergone 12-step treatment.[10] And when the Rand investigators re-examined their original findings and published their second report, the reported four-year abstinence rated dropped to 7%.[11]

Joan Mathews Larsen, in her book, *Alcoholism: The Biochemical Connection*, includes a chart showing the rates of two-year abstinence achieved through traditional treatment reported by various investigators[12]:

1. Gerald and Saneger (1962)   18%
2. Emrich (1974)   34%
3. Emrich (1975)   23%
4. Polich, (1980)   22%
5. Vaillant (1983)   19%
6. Powell (1985)   18%

On average, the percentages confirm Gorski's 75% relapse rate estimate. However, these statistics are still overly optimistic in the sense that they reflect abstinence/relapse rates within a one-to-two-year period. There is a parallel here with obesity, where most individuals who diet initially lose weight, but eventually gain it back in a relapse of sorts. The same is true of alcoholics and addicts who undergo 12-step treatment.[13]

To quote William Miller: "[R]elapse, as every alcohol professional knows, is a common phenomenon in addictive behaviors. Long-term follow-up data suggest that more than 90% of clients will drink again at some time after [abstinence-demanding] treatment."

There are a number of reasons why 12-step treatment effectiveness is typically exaggerated. Retired University of California professor Herbert Fingarette, in his book, *Heavy Drinking: The Myth of Alcoholism as a Disease*, cites biasing factors in treatment effectiveness studies:

1. Oftentimes, clients selected for hospital treatment studies are chosen because they appear well motivated and show no signs of "severe personality, physical, or neurological disorders."
2. Many patients who enter addictions treatment programs do so at a time when their drinking/drugging problems have "become particularly acute. In a sense, they have nowhere to go but up."
3. Many surveys include only the rate of improvement "for drinkers who complete the program," and dropouts "are not included . . . as failures."
4. In long-term follow-up studies, "persons who have died of causes related to resumed drinking (drugging) are often not counted among the graduates."
5. Addictions treatment programs (especially privately funded programs) draw their clients from high socioeconomic status groups. Such individuals typically show significantly higher rates of improvement than individuals from low socioeconomic status groups.
6. Many studies use a short time period in which to measure success, while the rate of relapse rises significantly subsequent to the first six months after leaving treatment.[14]

In addition, as George Vaillant states: "[I]nvestigators cannot forbid subjects to seek treatment elsewhere."[15] That is, in studies of specific programs, many patients are not counted as relapsed, because even though they did relapse, they then obtained treatment at a clinic or hospital not associated with the original treatment study.

This is a serious problem. An article in *Addictive Behaviors* notes:

Analysis of alcoholism treatment studies conducted between 1980 and 1992 shows that almost half of them are single-group studies. Researchers and patients in the studies are generally male. Most studies fail to provide information about patients and treatments, and lack control groups. Outcomes other than drinking are rarely studied.[16]

Chad Emrick, in a research report, *A Review of Psychologically Oriented Treatment of Alcoholism*, rates the relative effectiveness of a variety of treatment approaches encompassed in the Minnesota Model, and the effectiveness of addictions treatment. He writes:

A review of 384 studies of psychologically oriented treatment showed that differences in treatment methods did not significantly affect long-term outcome. Mean abstinence rates did not differ between treated and untreated alcoholics, but more treated than non-treated [individuals] improved, suggesting that formal treatment at least increases an alcoholic's chances of reducing his drinking problems.[17]

In essence, what Emrick is saying is that there appears to be no statistically significant correlation between traditional addictions treatment and abstinence outcomes. And any improvement shown by clients in the studies Emrick cites is in the area of clients moderating their alcohol intake—something which the treatment programs told them they could not do. As well, given that the studies Emrick cites were all conducted prior to 1975—that is, prior to the onset of mass coercion of individuals into treatment programs—it seems likely that clients would by and large have possessed that most important of positive biasing factors, motivation.

As well, more recent data, especially that provided by the massive, Census Bureau-conducted National Longitudinal Alcoholism Epidemiological Survey (NLAES) casts serious doubt on the belief that 12-step treatment does any good whatsoever. This survey of 43,000 individuals, of whom slightly over 10% at one time met at least three of the American Psychiatric Association's criteria of alcohol dependence, showed that more untreated than treated individuals recovered from their alcohol dependence, and that, 20 or more years after the onset of dependence, 20% of those who had been treated were still abusing alcohol, whereas only 10% of those who had never been treated were still abusing alcohol. In other words, in comparison with those who had never been treated, twice as many of the treated individuals were still drinking excessively.[18]

CASPAR

One of the programs that the NIAAA funded after passage of the Hughes Act was the Cambridge-Sommerville (Massachusetts) Program for Alcohol Rehabilitation (CASPAR). The CASPAR program established a network of alcoholism treatment clinics based on the Minnesota Model. These clinics provided 24-hour walk-in services which included medical treatment for detoxification, psychiatric consultation, outpatient addictions counseling, and 12-step support groups. During the 1970s, CASPAR treated 1000 new patients per year, conducted 2500 detoxifications per year, and scheduled 20,000 outpatient visits per year.

The program embraced the Jellinek disease concept of alcoholism, utilized paraprofessional ("recovering" alcoholic/addict) counselors, and relied heavily on AA principles and practices. One of those involved in administering the program, Harvard professor and AA General Service Board member George Vaillant, wrote: "I was working for the most exciting alcohol program in the world."[19]

In order to test the effectiveness of this "most exciting alcohol program," Vaillant and other investigators made a long-term comparison of the results achieved by 106 consecutive admissions to the CASPAR program with those of 245 "no treatment" individuals and 963 patients in four comparative alcoholism studies. Vaillant reported the results in his book, *The Natural History of Alcoholism*. His basic question was whether Minnesota Model treatment produced results superior to those of "spontaneous remission." After considering 40 years of clinical studies, including an eight-year longitudinal study of CASPAR patients, Vaillant determined that this treatment approach, in terms of long-term abstinence, produces results no better than the rate of spontaneous remission. Although Vaillant reported that Minnesota Model treatment appeared to produce dramatic effects at first, over the long run it made no difference whether "alcoholic" individuals were treated and attended AA, or went untreated and did not participate in AA. In either case, only about 5% of the alcoholic population surveyed by Vaillant managed to achieve sustained abstinence.

In addition, although the abstinence rate was the same for both groups, the 3% annual death rate for the treated alcoholics—a rate Vaillant termed "appalling"—was actually higher than the death rate in the no-treatment comparison group. Not only had "the most exciting alcohol program in the world" failed to arrest "the natural history of alcoholism," but, taking mortality rates into account, the overall effects of CASPAR's treatment program appear to be negative.

In the final analysis, the only positive aspect of the CASPAR program was, according to Vaillant, that it was "not interfering with the normal recovery process."[20]

Treatment and Mortality Rates

The high mortality rate of treated alcoholics within the Vaillant studies is supported by the results of a five-year mortality study of alcoholics conducted in conjunction with the DuPont Corporation. Of 76,687 employees of the corporation included in the survey, 922 were identified by physicians as alcoholic. The study included control groups in which each alcoholic employee was matched to another employee, known not to be alcoholic, by age, sex, payroll class (salary or hourly), and geographic location. The sample was segmented into three classifications: 1) known alcoholics; 2) suspected alcoholics; and 3) recovered/abstinent alcoholics.

The average yearly mortality rate for the known alcoholics was 3.2% (versus .74% for the matched comparison group); for the suspected alcoholics it was 1.8% (versus, again, .74% for the matched comparison group); and for the recovered alcoholics it was 2.5% (versus .86% for the matched comparison group).[21]

But a more recent survey of 12 long-term longitudinal studies of mortality rates of (for the most part) treated alcoholics found an average mortality rate of a still very high 2.15% per annum for the treated alcoholics, while the mortality rate in the single study of untreated alcoholics included in the survey was only 1.7% per annum, a lower figure than for all but one of the studies of treated alcoholics.[22]

Confirmation of Vaillant's Findings

A one-year study published in 1985 confirms Vaillant's 1983 findings concerning the ineffectiveness of 12-step treatment. In a controlled clinical study, alcoholics were segregated into three treatment groups: 1) those who received medication only (disulfiram [anatabuse] or chlordiazepoxide —drugs that produce physical discomfort when taken with alcohol); 2) those who received a complete addictions treatment program; and 3) those who received no treatment beyond a physical exam and a clinical interview once a month. The results were that the medication-only group had an 80% relapse rate; the treatment group had an 80% relapse rate; and the minimal-treatment group had a 74% relapse rate.

The study's authors concluded:

> Patients provided with a minimum of services showed as much improvement as those provided with extensive treatment over the same period of time. The ineffectiveness of the interventions could not be explained by differences in pretreatment alcoholism severity.[23]

A controlled study of chronic drunkenness offenders in San Diego showed similar results. Three hundred and one "chronic drunk offenders" were assigned as a condition of probation to either: 1) a clinical treatment program (type unspecified, although probably 12-step); 2) AA attendance; 3) a no-treatment control group. The results were that 68% of the treatment group were rearrested; 69% of the AA-attendance group were rearrested; but only 56% of the no-treatment controls were rearrested.[24]

The Treated Population

The Minnesota Model of addictions treatment projects a progressive and inevitable healing process of lifelong recovery. The key assumption underlying this projection is that abstinence from alcohol and other drugs along with the embracement of "spirituality" is all that is really needed to reach an unparalleled state of emotional and spiritual health—one that, as many "recovering" alcoholics and addicts humbly put it, makes them "better than well," that is, superior to "normies" who never had addictions problems. But the characteristics of the small minority of alcoholics/addicts who actually manage to achieve sustained abstinence—an obvious research target group—are seldom the focus of research attention.

Perhaps the reason that so little attention is paid to these individuals is the assumption within the treatment community, and within AA in particular, that sobriety/spirituality will automatically provide alcoholics/addicts with the solutions to their problems. In AA, the bald assumption is that following "the AA way of life" will inevitably "restore [alcoholics] to sanity."

But this is not necessarily true. In a research report called *The Abstinent Alcoholic*, researchers Donald Gerard, Gerhardt Saenger, and Renee Wile analyzed the abstinent population. The study included clients who had managed to achieve sobriety for up to nine years. On the basis of their findings and case studies, they divided the abstinent former alcoholics into four classifications:

1. Overtly Disturbed (54% of the total)
2. Inconspicuously Inadequate Personalities (24%)
3. Alcoholics Anonymous Successes (12%)
4. Independent Successes (10%)

The authors describe these groups as follows:

1. Overtly Disturbed . . . These ex-patients suffer with tension to a degree which concerns them; and/or they are angry, dissatisfied, or are resentful, projecting aggressive attitudes or ideas into their environment; and/or they are driven by anxiety so that they are restless, unable to relax, seeking to distract or sedate themselves from their conflicts by spending inordinate amounts of time at work or social activities of a community nature; and/or they are overtly psychiatrically ill, displaying disturbances of mood, thought, and behavior to a psychotic degree.

2. Inconspicuously Inadequate Personalities consist of those ex-patients whose total functioning is characterized by meagerness of their involvement in life and living. . . . There is nothing grossly "wrong" in their lives. They are not presently likely to go to jail or to a mental hospital, nor are they very troubled. On the other hand, there is no positive sense of excitement, purpose, or interest in life. . . .

3. AA Successes . . . It is evident that they are as dependent on AA as they were before on alcohol . . . They are very active in AA. Some of them spend all or practically all of their free time at AA or in 12-step work. Conversely, they have little or no social life apart from AA. . . .

4. Independent Successes . . . These ex-patients have achieved a state of self-respecting independence, of personal growth, and self-realization. They differ from the first subgroup in that they do not appear disturbed . . . ; they differ from the second subgroup in that they are more alive and interesting as human beings . . . ; and they differ from the third subgroup in that their efforts at self-realization are independent rather than institutionally supported. . . .[25]

It certainly appears that the AA promise that "working the steps" (the centerpiece of 12-step treatment) will make individuals "happily and usefully whole"[26] was not fulfilled for the fully 90% of the individuals studied who were—after treatment, and, presumably, continued participation in AA—either overtly disturbed (54%), had "inadequate" personalities (24%), or were "AA successes" (12%).

---

1. *Getting Better Inside Alcoholics Anonymous*, by Nan Robertson. New York: Wm. Morrow, 1988, p. 217–220.
2. Ibid., p. 219.
3. *Alcohol Problems: A Report to the Nation.* National Institute on Alcohol Abuse and Alcoholism. New York: Oxford University Press, 1967, pp. 191–192.
4. *Addiction, Change and Choice: The New View of Alcoholism*, by Vince Fox. Tucson, AZ: See Sharp Press, 1993, pp. 42–43.
5. Ibid., p. 57.
6. Ibid., p. 142.
7. *The Progression and Recovery of the Alcoholic*, by Parkside Medical Corporation, 1988.
8. "Alcoholism: Disease or Addiction?", by G. Alan Marlatt and Terence Gorski. *Professional Counselor*, October 1996, p. 294.
9. *The Natural History of Alcoholism*, by George Vaillant. Cambridge, MA: Harvard University Press, 1983, p. 294.
10. "Chemical Dependency and Mental Health: Avoiding a Shotgun Merger," by Terence Gorski. *Behavioral Health Management*, Volume 14, January 1994, p. 22.

11. *The Course of Alcoholism Four Years After Treatment*, by J. Michael Polich, David J. Armor, and Harriet B. Braiker. New York: John Wiley & Sons, 1980, p. 169.
12. *Alcoholism: The Biochemical Connection*, by Joan Matthews Larsen and Keith Sehnert. New York: Random House, 1992, p. 15.
13. *Handbook of Alcoholism Treatment Approaches: Effective Alternatives (Second Edition)*, Reid Hester and William Miller, eds. Boston: Allyn & Bacon, 1995, p. 92.
14. *Heavy Drinking: The Myth of Alcoholism as a Disease*, by Herbert Fingarette. Berkeley: University of California Press, 1988, pp. 80–83.
15. Vaillant, op. cit., p. 188.
16. "Alcoholism Treatment Outcome Studies, 1980–1992: The Nature of the Research," by Anthony Floyd et al. *Addictive Behaviors*, July/August 1996, Volume 21, Number 4, p. 413.
17. "A Revew of Psychologically Oriented Treatment of Alcoholism," by Chad Emrick. *Journal of Studies on Alcohol*, Volume 36, 1975, pp. 88–108.
18. "Correlates of Past-Year Status Among Treated and Untreated Persons with Former Alcohol Dependence: United States, 1992," by Deborah Dawson. *Alcoholism: Clinical & Experimental Research*, Volume 20, 1996, pp. 771–779.
19. Vaillant, op. cit., p. 350.
20. Ibid., p. 152.
21. "A Five-Year Mortality Study of Alcoholics," by Sidney Pell and C.A. D'Alonzo. *Journal of Occupational Medicine*, Volume 15 Number 2, February 1973, pp. 120–125.
22. "The Long-Term Course of Treated Alcoholism: I. Mortality, Relapse, and Remission Rates and Comparisons with Community Controls," by Finney, John and Moos, Rudolf. *Journal of Studies on Alcohol*, Volume 52, 1991, pp. 44–54.
23. "Comparison of Three Outpatient Treatment Interventions: A Twelve-Month Follow-Up of Male Alcoholics," by Barbara Powell, et al. *Journal of Studies on Alcohol*, Volume 46, 1985, pp. 309–312.
24. "A Controlled Experiment on the Use of Court Probation for Drunk Arrests," by Keith Ditman, et al. *American Journal of Psychiatry*, August 1967, pp. 64–67.
25. "The Abstinent Alcoholic," by Donald Gerard, Gerhardt Saenger, and Renee Wile. *Archives of General Psychiatry*, Volume 6, 1962, pp. 99–110.
26. *Twelve Steps and Twelve Traditions*, by Bill Wilson. New York: Alcoholics Anonymous World Services, 1953, p. 15.

8

Reasons for 12-Step Dominance
of the Treatment Industry

The Anomalous Nature of 12-Step Treatment

In a 1993 *Journal of Substance Abuse Treatment* article, authors Emil Chiauzzi and Steven Liljegren describe the treatment of addictions as an "anomaly" in the health care field.[1] In fact, it is an "anomaly" in more than one sense. One very striking illustration of this is that the predominant treatment modality in the U.S. and Canada (12-step treatment) is almost entirely unsupported by the best available scientific evidence (controlled studies), while well-supported, less expensive alternative treatments go almost unused.

A second example of the "anomalous" nature of 12-step addictions treatment is that its practitioners *routinely* disregard the almost universal (in other areas of medicine) principle of "informed consent." Under the principle of informed consent, treatment providers are supposed to explain the nature of a proposed treatment, explain its advantages and disadvantages versus other forms of treatment or no treatment, and obtain the patient's consent before proceeding with treatment. But in the addictions field, treatment providers rarely explain the nature of the proposed treatment; they almost never accurately explain the advantages and disadvantages of 12-step treatment versus other forms of treatment (or no treatment); and they routinely impose their favored form of treatment expressly *against* their clients' stated desires.

In any other area of medicine, such practices would quickly raise howls of protest, which would very likely result in immediate cessation of such practices, and would quite likely also lead to disciplinary action against those engaging in them. But in the addictions treatment field, such "anomalous" practices are the *norm*. They are almost universally accepted as business as usual, both by those in the addictions treatment field and by the public.[2]

How did such practices come to be so widely accepted? One way in which such practices have come to be virtually unquestioned is that the vast majority of treatment facilities (well over 90% of which are 12-step providers) routinely assure the public that their method of treatment is the most or the only effective form of treatment, and that it *must* be imposed upon "alcoholics" or "addicts" because they are *in denial*. (Needless to say, this is a very convenient argument for treatment providers: if an individual admits that he's an alcoholic or addict, he is automatically labeled as such; but if he denies being an alcoholic or addict, he's *in denial*—strong evidence that he *is* an alcoholic or addict. In the first case, the self-admitted alcoholic/addict will often voluntarily submit to treatment; in the second case, treatment must be imposed for the individual's "own good.")

As well, over the years 12-step true believers have set up a number of "educational" and "medical" front groups which promote the "anomalous" practices of the treatment industry. The two most prominent of these front groups are, as previously mentioned, the American Society of Addiction Medicine and the National Council on Alcoholism and Drug Dependence.[3] Such groups routinely promote not only 12-step ideology and 12-step groups, but also the most extreme violation imaginable of the principle of informed consent—coercive "interventions." These organizations provide the treatment industry's "anomalous" practices with a scientific and medical gloss. The overabundance of lazy, uninformed reporters and hidden 12-step members in the media are only too happy to treat the pronouncements of these 12-step front groups as "news," and the "anomalous" practices they promote as normal and necessary.

Psychic Surrender

But one suspects that other factors are at work here beyond the domination of the addictions treatment field by true believers and the influence of their very slick propaganda machine. One suspects that the widespread abandonment of individual responsibility and self-direction is also a primary factor in the acceptance of the 12-step industry's coercive, ineffective, "anomalous" practices.

In the September/October 1983 issue of *The Humanist*, in an article entitled "Psychic Surrender: America's Creeping Paralysis," author Michael Scott Cain describes the manner in which a great many people abdicate control of their lives to a variety of cult-like organizations. He writes:

> Psychic surrender, a malady that's becoming progressively stronger in many aspects of our culture, can be defined as the act of turning complete control of your life, all responsibility for your total existence, over to someone you perceive as stronger and more capable than you.

Scott Cain's article was prophetic; it was a harbinger of things to come. During the 1980s and early 1990s, as the AA movement expanded, ever more individuals within our society were turning their lives and wills over to a "higher power."

Responsibility for Treatment Failures

"Psychic surrender" programs, such as AA, are inherently "safe"—for treatment providers, if not for clients. Twelve-step therapists and treatment programs adopt the attitude exemplified in the AA slogan, "It works if you work it!" That is, if clients properly "work" the 12-step program, they will recover. If they don't recover, they weren't properly "working" the program. In other words, the treatment itself is perfect if properly "worked." This places all responsibility for success upon the client; if the client fails, neither the treatment provider nor the treatment itself bear any responsibility whatsoever.

When a client "fails," due, of course, to not properly working the program, the typical prescription given to him is to attend more meetings. If he does this and still relapses, the relapse was due to his improperly working the program, perhaps, for example, by "leaving something out" of his fifth step.

In a field as rife with treatment failures as addictions treatment, one can well understand the allure for treatment providers of this blame-the-client approach.

Ironically, one can consider this attitude as a pronounced form of "denial." Authors Pia Mellody, Andrea Wells Miller, and Keith Miller, in their book, *Facing Codependence*, write: "Perfectionism is dysfunctional." Like the majority of people within the ACoA and codependency movement, they acknowledge the damaging effects of perfectionism. How ironic it is, then, that a majority of these individuals also advocate the 12-step approach to addictions recovery, an approach which is de facto considered by most of its adherents as perfect (in that it *always* works if properly "worked").

Further explanation of the attitudes of those within the treatment industry was provided at a conference sponsored by the National Association for Children of Alcoholics. A workshop entitled, "COAs Working in the Alcoholism Field: Return to Family of Origin," presented by Susan Nobleman, described how addictions treatment counselors routinely enter the addictions treatment field. According to Nobleman, 71% of addictions professionals enter the field as a result of personal need for addictions treatment. "The vast majority of the sample study did not plan in the sense of any schooling or special training for this job."[4] Instead, they enter into an addictions treatment program and are later recruited into the profession by "recovering" professionals. This is still another anomaly, and one which largely explains the two previously mentioned anomalies (the use of scientifically unsupported therapies and the disregard of the principle of informed consent): Addictions treatment is the only treatment field in which clients and therapists are drawn from the same "dysfunctional" pool of individuals.

This is the source of the often extreme pro-12-step bias within the addictions treatment community. A great many 12-step addictions treatment providers believe, literally—as they were told repeatedly in treatment and in AA—that their lives were saved by the 12-step program, and that without it they would suffer "jails, institutions, or death." In essence, true believers recruit other true believers, and the system perpetuates itself.

This creates an obvious conflict of interest for 12-step treatment providers, in that they're ethically bound to provide their clients with the most effective treatment available. But they don't do this, and instead force ineffective 12-step treatment down the throats of their clients because of *their* (the treatment providers') personal beliefs and experiences.

Transference of Family Dynamics

Still, the fact that a majority of addictions counselors are "recovering" alcoholics or addicts does not fully explain the behavior of these counselors. The remainder of the explanation was provided by Joseph C. Kern, director of Alcoholism Treatment Services in Nassau County, New York. In his workshop entitled "The Dysfunctional Alcoholism Agency," Kern explains that at least 80% to 85% of individuals working in alcoholism treatment facilities were raised in alcoholic homes, and within an agency structure replicate the lifestyle of their families of origin. He goes on to explain the patterns of behavior associated with a dysfunctional alcoholic family unit using as backdrop the work of author-therapist Sharon Wegscheider-Cruse. The alcoholic family's behavioral/belief patterns are described as follows:

1. The dependent's use of alcohol is the most important thing in the family's life.

2. Alcohol is not the cause of the family's problems.

3. Someone or something else caused the alcoholic's dependency; he is not responsible.

4. The status quo must be maintained at all costs.

5. Everyone in the family must be an enabler.

6. No one may discuss what is really going on in the family, either with one another or with outsiders.

7. No one may say what he is really feeling.

Kern indicates that within the agency structure many staff members manifest these patterns in a modified form, as follows:

1. Instead of alcohol use being the "most important thing" in group life, agency staff view the alcoholism/addictions field as the "most important thing." Symptoms of this are that staff members manifest a "compulsive dedication" toward the field and exhibit a "self-righteous" attitude in regard to their profession. A majority of staff believe that because others outside the field of addictions treatment have not "lived the disease" and lack personal experience with treatment and recovery, they are not fully capable of understanding addictions and/or treatment. Many staff members believe that they alone know the "secrets" of addiction and as a result hold "the keys to the kingdom" in a spiritual-religious sense.

2. "Alcohol is not the cause of the family's problems" is translated within an agency structure to, "The agency, the staff, and the collective belief system are not the problem." In the event that the agency encounters treatment difficulties, the staff typically blame external factors or forces. Staff members tend to be "arrogant," "self-righteous," and "lack the ability to be introspective." Kern indicates that many agencies contain staff members who avoid "corrective feedback," manifest a "rigidity of thought," and exhibit "classic codependency symptoms."

3. "Someone or something else caused the alcoholic's dependency; he is not responsible," becomes, "Factors outside the agency, agency staff, and their collective belief system and treatment practices are the cause of any treatment failures." Staff members tend to maintain the "existential position" that they are "right" and beyond reproach. The problem concerning agency shortcomings stems from the fact that those outside the agency structure do not understand the nature of alcoholism and do not conform to the agency's collective belief system.

4. "The status quo must be maintained at all costs" is translated to, "Everyone within the agency structure must be loyal only to this agency or cause, and must cover up mistakes." Thus staff members tend to resist change, new programs, and new approaches.

5. "Everyone in the family must be an enabler" is translated to, "Everyone within the agency . . . must be loyal only to this agency or cause." Kern indicates that many staff members "cover up mistakes," do not "confront incompetence" exhibited by staff members, manifest a "we can do it on our own" mentality, and seldom seek outside assistance in dealing with internal problems. Kern also states that a relatively large number of agencies contains staff members who are "clinically depressed," and that "rescuing and excusing those who cannot meet expectations" is common.

6. "No one may discuss what is really going on in the family, either with one another or with outsiders," becomes, "Don't be honest and problem solve." Kern indicates that many staff members tend to become "isolated" and have little contact with others outside their belief system; because of this, many staff members avoid continued education and hold "rigid, distorted perceptions" of reality.

7. "No one may say what he is really feeling" is translated to, "Don't express a direct feeling—especially anger." Kern notes that this causes "resentment" and produces "lack of clear, honest dialogue between agencies and constituency groups."

In addition, Kern describes many of the professionals within the addictions treatment field as being as psychologically unhealthy as their clients. He notes the response of agency staff to staff members who do not conform to the norms of the common belief system, or who attempt to expose and correct obvious flaws. Such individuals are normally forced to leave, a process which even has a descriptive term: "freezing out." This entails a variety of passive-aggressive behaviors and the avoidance of direct confrontation; the nonconforming individual is simply shunned out of the group or agency. Criticism of the belief system is not tolerated, and maintenance of the status quo is more important than efficacy.[5] In a subsequent article Kern refers to this as the "Groupthink phenomenon."[6]

It's also pertinent that Kern is not alone in his estimate of the percentage of workers in the alcoholism field whose families of origin are alcoholic. In a 1995 article, Robin Walter also estimates that 80% of workers in the helping professions come from such backgrounds.[7]

12-Step Expansionism

As the 12-step movement expanded to encompass an ever-wider variety of "diseases" (that is, unhealthy behaviors), many within the recovery movement projected their view of reality onto the population at large. In essence, they reframed reality to conform to the norms of the monolithic 12-step belief system. This process can be aptly described as evangelical in nature. Each new carbon-copy program was part of the larger 12-step religious/spiritual system, and application of the program became entirely formulaic: any self-defeating or compulsive behavior called for the same one-size-fits-all prescription—yet another 12-step program, the core of which differed from the cores of the other 12-step programs only in single terms in the first and twelfth steps.

Perhaps the most extreme example of this one-size-fits-all approach is the "codependence" phenomenon. According to leading "experts" on the topic, 95% or 96% of the population suffer from this "disease." The remedy? You guessed it—another 12-step program (Codependents Anonymous) and more 12-step "therapy."

Another example of this expansionist approach is the broadening of the definition of "adult children of alcoholics." According to "experts" in this field, the ACoA pattern is passed down within families from generation to generation, so you can suffer from this disorder even if your parents *weren't* alcoholic; you can suffer from it if one of your grandparents or even one of your great-grandparents was alcoholic. Again, this encompasses probably a good majority of the population.

ACoA/Codependency Issues

One of the most peculiar aspects of the overall 12-step movement is that those most intimately involved in it, addictions treatment personnel (who come overwhelmingly from alcoholic families), are among those most afflicted by ACoA/codependency issues, and that—as evidenced by their behaviors and attitudes in their workplaces—they are also among the most unable or unwilling to deal with those issues. Instead of being independent adults, many of them are every bit as dependent upon the 12-steps and 12-step programs as their clients. For example, at professional addictions conferences, workshops, and seminars it is not at all uncommon for 12-step support groups to be made available for the benefit of the professionals in attendance. This is almost always done to the exclusion of any other type of support group. The real question here is why is it necessary to provide such support groups to professionals at all?

An answer can be found in the nature and scope of the 12 steps themselves. The manner in which they nurture dependence within their believers is very much a reflection of the conditions in alcoholic homes and families. One can glimpse what these conditions are through an early, restrictive definition of the term "codependence." Prior to having been expanded, convoluted, and rendered meaningless, the term did have meaning in a limited clinical setting for a specific population. In her book, *Choice Making*, author Sharon Wegscheider-Cruse quotes Robert Subby, director of Family Systems, Inc. Subby describes codependence as:

> . . . an emotional, psychological, behavioral condition that develops as a result of an individual's prolonged exposure to, and practice of, a set of oppressive rules—rules which prevent the open expression of feeling, as well as the direct discussion of personal and interpersonal problems.

Using this as a base, Wegscheider-Cruse provides her own definition:

> Codependency is a specific condition that is characterized by preoccupation and extreme dependence (emotionally, socially, and sometimes physically), on a person or object. Eventually, this dependence on another person becomes a pathological condition that affects the codependent in all other relationships.[8]

This definition is significant in that it perfectly describes the relationship of 12-step group members (including 12-step professionals) to 12-step programs. It's also worth noting that because alcoholics/addicts are permanently "recovering" but never "recover," the dependency inherent in the 12 steps is a dependency for life. Given that a majority of professionals within the addictions treatment field have had a personal and intimate relationship with addiction, and are members of 12-step groups, it's not surprising that they lack the emotional-psychological detachment necessary to maintain objectivity and critical thinking when providing treatment, as well as the open-mindedness to objectively assess new scientific data.

William Talley, founder of the now-defunct Turning Points in Sobriety, one of the first attempts at a national, non-12-step alcohol self-help program, points out the inherent problems/contradictions in a program which substitutes one dependency (and a life-long one at that) for another:

> All psychotherapies should and usually do come to an end after a period of time, ideally when the therapeutic goals have been met. Indeed, termination of therapy should be one of the goals. . . . Keeping the illness/addiction central in one's life long after a healthy period of abstinence and equanimity has been achieved is tantamount to perpetuating the illness . . . since old memories, feelings and reactions are or can be continually renewed. . . . Recovered addicts who become professionals in the treatment of addiction . . . are themselves at risk of reactivating addictive reactions and ultimately relapses. They may in many cases be considered as carriers of disease, whose influence on patients/clients may be detrimental. . . . Any program, whether secular or religious, which has as its primary operating assumption and its chief observable characteristic long-term, indefinite dependency is not a therapeutic program but a religious or social institution.[9]

Somewhere within the quagmire of the AA movement and the myriad of 12-step programs associated with it, the meaning of the word *recovery* was lost. By definition, recovery is a retrieval and reclamation process, not a surrender and abdication of individual independence and personal power. The process of recovery or regaining emotional balance and well-being entails independence from addictive chemicals, compulsive behaviors, therapists, and recovery groups. To transfer dependence on chemically addictive substances to emotional-psychological dependence on a group or recovery program is not recovery in the true sense of the word.

Conclusions

This is the nature of the problem. The overwhelming majority of addictions counselors in the United States are drawn from the ranks of the severely addicted. The result is an informal and unwritten screening process, in which only the small minority who respond enthusiastically to the AA/Minnesota Model of treatment and to AA itself are actively recruited into the profession. In essence, true believers recruit other true believers. In addition, as Joseph Kern points out, those who break rank and do not conform to the institutionalized 12-step belief system are "frozen out" and induced to resign. This is understandable given that many, probably most, American addictions counselors quite literally believe that strict adherence to 12-step programs is a matter of life or death—that they literally owe their lives to AA (NA, etc.)—and therefore those who do not share their belief system are seen as a dire threat.

This produces an obvious conflict of interest: what may serve the needs of the "recovering" individuals doing the counseling does not necessarily meet the needs of their clients. When treatment providers are drawn from the ranks of 12-step recovery groups (or some other program), this creates a bias toward that approach and a resistance toward alternatives. The field might be greatly improved if individuals with a history of addictive behavior and/or parental alcoholism/addiction were screened out. At present, many of the individuals who are engaged in addictions counseling and are also involved in a 12-step program would be positively traumatized if they were forced to abandon the 12-step approach for other more effective alternatives. On the other hand, individuals without a history of addictive behavior and familial addiction and no emotional-psychological attachment to any particular program or treatment approach could shift gears relatively easily. But at present more than 70% of addictions counselors are drawn from the under 10% of the population with addictions problems, and 80% to 85% of those counselors also come from alcoholic families of origin.

The relationship between addictions counselors, therapists, addictions treatment facilities, and AA and other 12-step groups is symbiotic. Treatment facilities provide AA with a steady stream of new members and a huge amount of literature sales, while AA provides treatment facilities with a steady stream of true-believing, low-paid addictions counselors. AA also provides counselors and treatment facilities with a program which places all responsibility on the client, and none on the counselors or therapy: if clients fail, it's due to their not properly working "the program."

Twelve-step facilities quite often use not only a strict 12-step approach, but restrict reading matter to only AA and NA "conference-approved" literature. This in effect keeps 12-step clients in the dark and protects therapists from criticism. It places therapists in the position of being one-up on 12-step clients. This one-size-fits-all approach also simplifies therapy for providers. Rather than having to sort through a variety of approaches and programs to find the ones most likely to help specific clients, patients can be (and are) processed in factory-like manner. Never mind that precious few of them derive much benefit from the treatment provided.

To sum up, (drawing on this and previous chapters) 12-step treatment is dominant in the United States for many reasons:

1) It was established at a time of near vacuum in the treatment and research of addictions;

2) Its foundation (Jellinek's disease concept) was developed at a highly prestigious university and was not subjected to any real, sustained criticism for decades after it was expounded;

3) The 12-step treatment industry (and AA) has a very slick, effective "educational" and "medical" propaganda apparatus (e.g., NCADD and ASAM);

4) The media are lazy and tend to uncritically report the self-serving statements of that apparatus as "news";

5) With an AA member as its sponsor, the U.S. Congress passed the Hughes Act, which has funneled billions of dollars into the 12-step addictions treatment industry;

6) The treatment industry is overwhelmingly staffed by 12-step true believers who recruit other true believers into the profession, and who "freeze out" dissidents;

7) Because of untreated psychological problems, a great many treatment personnel have an extreme, unhealthy emotional dependence upon 12-step ideology and 12-step groups, and therefore tend to see alternative approaches to addictions treatment as a threat to their own lives and identities;

8) The 12-step treatment industry and its propaganda apparatus attempt (for the most part successfully) to thwart the development and implementation of alternative approaches.

---

1. "Taboo Topics in Addiction Treatment: An Empirical Review of Clinical Folklore," by Emil J. Chiauzzi and Steven Liljgren. *Journal of Substance Abuse Treatment*, Volume 10, 1993, pp. 303–316.
2. See *Resisting 12-Step Coercion: How to Fight Forced Participation in AA, NA, or 12-Step Treatment*, by Stanton Peele, Charles Bufe, and Archie Brodsky. Tucson, AZ: See Sharp Press, 2000, chapters 2 and 5 for further discussion of these "anomalous" practices in the treatment field.
3. See *Alcoholics Anonymous: Cult or Cure? (Second Edition)*, by Charles Bufe. Tucson, AZ: See Sharp Press, 1998, chapter 8, for further analysis of the influence of the NCADD and ASAM.
4. "COAs Working in the Alcoholism Field: Return to Family of Origin," workshop presented by Susan Nobleman. National Association for Children of Alcoholics, Northeast Regional Conference, November 14–15, 1986 (lecture—audio cassette).
5. "The Dysfunctional Alcoholism Agency," workshop presented by Joseph C. Kern. National Association for Children of Alcoholics, Northeast Regional Conference, November 14–15, 1986 (lecture—audio cassette).
6. "Adult Children of Alcoholics as Professionals in the Alcoholism Field," by Joseph C. Kern. In Robert J. Ackerman, ed., *Growing in the Shadow*. Pompano Beach, FL: Health Communications, 1986, pp. 197–207.
7. "Codependence? Nonsense," by Robin R. Walter. *RN*, February 1995, Volume 58, p. 80.
8. *Choice Making*, by Sharon Wegscheider-Cruse. Pompano Beach, FL: Health Communications, 1985, p. 2.
9. "Secular Heresy: Should Peer Support End," by William Talley. *Recovery*, June/July 1984, pp. 3–5.

9

What Works?

Evaluating the Evidence—
Controlled and Uncontrolled Studies

The full irrationality of the devotion to the 12-step approach among American treatment providers (described in the previous chapter) can only be fully appreciated when one looks at the best scientific evidence regarding treatment efficacy, controlled studies. Twelve-step advocates are very reluctant to do this (let alone act on the logical conclusions to be drawn from such studies), and instead rely upon the weak evidence provided by uncontrolled studies and anecdotal evidence. A good example of this is Harvard professor and Alcoholics Anonymous General Service Board member George Vaillant's discussion of the efficacy of AA in his book, *The Natural History of Alcoholism Revisited*. Vaillant devotes 16 pages to the discussion of AA's efficacy and considers uncontrolled studies at length, yet he does not even mention the only two controlled studies ever conducted of AA's efficacy.[1] (As we'll see below, both studies reported negative results.) Vaillant even writes as if these studies do not exist, stating, "controlled studies of AA have proven too difficult to carry out"[2]—even though one of the controlled studies is listed in his book's bibliography.

Why is this so bad? Why is the disregard by AA's advocates of controlled studies and their reliance instead on uncontrolled studies and testimonials so reprehensible? An important article by Holder et al. in the *Journal of Studies on Alcohol* puts the matter well:

Prior reviews of the alcoholism treatment outcome literature have suggested that evidence from controlled clinical trials is considerably more consistent than the cumulative evidence of uncontrolled case studies and group designs. Positive uncontrolled reports can be found for virtually every treatment that has been tried for alcoholism, including psychosurgery, respiratory paralysis and the administration of LSD. . . . Positive or negative outcomes may be attributable not only to the treatment offered, but to a host of confounding factors including patient selection criteria, expectancies, additional treatment components and posttreatment factors. Uncontrolled trials also offer no basis for comparison of outcomes. Is a 40% success rate a triumph or a disgrace compared with what would be expected from no treatment or alternative treatments? . . . Controlled trials in general, and randomized clinical trials in particular, are commonly employed as the standard of evidence for specific effectiveness of medical treatments.[3]

So, 12-step advocates ignore standard medical procedure by disregarding the best available scientific evidence on the efficacy of treatment for what they insist is a chronic, life-threatening disease. Instead, based on personal conviction, they grab at whatever evidence is available, no matter how weak—uncontrolled studies, anecdotal evidence, even testimonials—and continue to advocate and apply an ineffective treatment.

Treatment Efficacy—Meta-Analyses

But what does the best evidence regarding the efficacy of 12-step (and other) treatment say? Over the past few decades, over 200 studies which have used control and/or comparison groups have been conducted of treatment efficacy. During the 1990s, three meta-analyses of these studies of treatment efficacy were published.[4][5][6] All three of the meta-analyses reached very similar conclusions:

1. Twelve-step treatment is, as a whole, ineffective;

2. The various components of 12-step treatment are themselves ineffective;

3. Twelve-step (especially inpatient) treatment is among the most expensive types of treatment;

4. Several cognitive-behavioral treatments are effective;

5. These effective cognitive-behavioral treatments are all either low cost or very low cost.

Of the three meta-analyses, perhaps the most important was that conducted by William Miller and Reid Hester, which appears in their book, *Handbook of Alcoholism Treatment Approaches*, along with detailed descriptions of a number of different therapies. Miller and Hester include a comprehensive evidence score (CES) which is based on both the quality of individual studies' methodology (such things as randomization [or lack of it] of subjects, follow-up completion rate, follow-up length, whether or not dropouts were enumerated, etc.) and on the strength of the studies' conclusions. A positive CES score for a treatment modality indicates that positive treatment outcomes have been observed and verified in controlled studies; and the higher the score the better the evidence of treatment efficacy. Conversely, a negative CES score for a treatment modality indicates that there is positive evidence of *lack* of treatment efficacy; and the lower the score, the greater the evidence of inefficacy. The authors also included an estimated base cost (in 1990 dollars) of delivery of the individual therapies.

In all, the authors evaluated the evidence of efficacy for 43 treatment modalities. Two of the types studied were apparently conventional 12-step therapy: "Milieu Therapy" and "Unspecified 'Standard' Treatment." (It's reasonable to conclude that "Milieu Therapy" corresponds to 12-step inpatient treatment, given that *The National Treatment Center Study Summary Report* states that 96% of inpatient facilities in the United States are 12-step facilities; and it's equally reasonable to conclude that "Unspecified 'Standard' Treatment" corresponds to 12-step treatment, given that the same *Summary Report* states that over 90% of treatment facilities in the U.S. are 12-step facilities.) Six additional types of evaluated therapies are standard components of 12-step treatment. They are:

1. Alcoholics Anonymous. AA typically forms the heart of both inpatient and outpatient 12-step treatment, with clients at inpatient facilities routinely being forced to "work" the first three to five AA steps. The goal of both types of treatment is to introduce the client to AA and to influence him or her to maintain lifetime AA membership following treatment.

2. Confrontational Counseling. In this form of "counseling" an individual is attacked during group therapy, almost always by the facilitator and often by other group members as well. The purpose of this "counseling" is to break through "denial" by shattering the target's ego until he or she "cracks."

3. Videotape Self-Confrontation. This involves the videotaping of alcohol abusers while they are intoxicated and the subsequent forced viewing of these tapes by the alcohol abusers. This became a common component of Minnesota Model treatment in the 1970s.

4. Psychotherapy. Group and individual psychotherapy is commonly employed within treatment centers in order to deal with the psychological aspects of addiction. Exploratory, or insight-oriented, therapy is typically provided to patients. Since the Minnesota Model maintains that alcoholism is a disease, psychotherapy in conjunction with the 12 steps is a common component of conventional treatment.

5. General Alcoholism Counseling. Advice, guidance, and applied psychological counseling about alcohol problems is typically provided by paraprofessionals, who are usually "recovering" alcoholics/addicts who have obtained certification to provide treatment in the addictions field. The training for such certification is generally of short duration, and the amount of time spent and work necessary to receive such certification does not even approach that necessary to receive a liberal arts bachelors degree.

6. Educational Lectures/Films. The purpose of such lectures and films is, almost invariably, to indoctrinate patients into belief in the disease model of alcoholism/addiction. Patients are informed that they are victims of a chronic, progressive, life-threatening disease for which there is no cure. They are also told that "denial" is a basic element of their "disease," and that attendance at an appropriate treatment facility and subsequent lifelong participation in Alcoholics Anonymous are essential to their recovery.

The following simplified chart is derived from that provided by Miller and Hester.[7] It shows only about a third of the treatment modalities (though all of the 12-step components) and reports only the cumulative evidence scores (CES) and base costs in 1990 dollars. Therapies here are ranked in descending order of effectiveness, with the most effective at the top of the list:

TREATMENT MODALITY	CES	COST
Brief Intervention	+239	46
Social Skills Training	+128	270
Motivational Enhancement	+87	46
Community Reinforcement Approach	+80	492
Behavior Contracting	+73	164
Self-Help Manual	+33	20
Cognitive Therapy	+22	433
Milieu Therapy	−41	1960
Alcoholics Anonymous	−52	0
Unspecified "Standard" Treatment	−53	738
Videotape Self-Confrontation	−77	548
Confrontational Counseling	−125	375
Psychotherapy	−127	4050
General Alcoholism Counseling	−214	738
Educational Lectures/Films	−239	135

There are a number of things of interest here. First, *all eight of the rated standard 12-step treatment approaches show negative evidence of efficacy*, with the last four listed being the lowest rated therapies out of all 43 modalities surveyed by Miller and Hester. Second, four of these ineffective modalities (Psychotherapy, Milieu Therapy, Unspecified "Standard" Treatment, and General Alcoholism Counseling) are the four *highest in cost* of all 43 rated modalities. Third, all five of the top-rated therapy modalities (Brief Intervention, Social Skills Training, Motivational Enhancement, Community Reinforcement Approach, and Behavior Contracting) are all cognitive-behavioral approaches. Fourth, all of these effective approaches fall in the very low to moderate price range in relation to the other therapies studied.

But perhaps the most striking thing about all of this is that *ineffective, expensive treatment approaches are the most common type used in the United States, while effective, low-cost approaches go almost unused in this country.*

Effective Treatments

The effective, top-rated, low-to-moderate-cost, cognitive-behavioral approaches are described by Stanton Peele and Charles Bufe in *Resisting 12-Step Coercion* as follows:

Brief Intervention / Motivational Enhancement. Brief intervention shares elements with motivational enhancement . . . in that the patient and the therapist create a mutually agreed-upon goal. The first step in creating this goal is often an objective assessment of the person's drinking habits, or a comparison of his or her drinking levels with community standards, or else a comparison with optimum levels of drinking for health purposes. In brief intervention, the goal is usually reduced drinking; in motivational enhancement, it is either reduced drinking or total abstinence. The key is to allow patients to select a goal that is consistent with their own values and that they thus "own" as an expression of their genuine desires.

In a brief-intervention session, the health-care worker simply sums up the goal: "So, we agree you will reduce your drinking from 42 drinks a week to 20, no more than four on a given night." Motivational enhancement is a bit more subtle: the therapist nudges without directing, by responding to the patient's own values and desire for change. . . .

Social Skills Training (SST). The basic premise of social skills training is that alcohol/drug-abuse clients lack basic skills in dealing with work, family, other interpersonal relationships, and their own emotions. Thus, they benefit from training in areas such as communications skills (including giving and receiving criticism, listening, and conversational skills), conflict resolution, drink-refusal, assertiveness, and expressing feelings. [SST typically utilizes both group settings (for skills training) and one-on-one counseling.]

Community Reinforcement Approach (CRA). This is . . . a moderately low-cost form of outpatient treatment; it was devised and first tested over a quarter-century ago; . . . every [controlled] study of its efficacy—six, so far—has shown extremely encouraging results; and it is not in use as a regular form of treatment at a single one of the 15,000 alcoholism treatment centers in the United States . . .

The basic premise of the community reinforcement approach—most often a one-on-one therapy, although it can be used in group settings—is that alcohol abuse does not occur in a vacuum, that it is highly influenced by marital, family, social, and economic factors (the exact opposite of the AA/12-step premise that alcoholism [or drug addiction] is a purely *individual* disease that exists independently of social conditions). CRA attempts to help the client improve his or her life in all of these areas, in addition to giving up drinking (or using drugs). Thus, a CRA program will typically include the following components: 1) communications skills training; 2) problem-solving training; 3) help finding employment; 4) social counseling (that is, encouraging the client to develop nondrinking relationships); 5) recreational counseling (that is, encouraging or helping the client to find rewarding nondrinking activities); and 6) marital therapy. Other treatment components are sometimes used—for example, disulfiram (Antabuse), drink-refusal training, or rewarding the client materially for abstinence—but these six components form the core of the CRA approach.[8]

Because, sadly, these treatment approaches are so little used in the United States, we'll cut short their discussion here and move on to perhaps the hottest button in American addictions treatment, moderate drinking as a treatment goal for alcohol abusers.

Moderate Drinking Therapies

One of the most noticeable aspects of addiction treatment in the United States is the near total absence of therapies with moderate drinking (rather than abstinence) as the goal. This is due primarily to the influence of the disease model of alcoholism, which implicitly demands abstinence as the only acceptable goal for anyone with an alcohol problem. Disease-model advocates often make this demand explicit.

This is unfortunate for several reasons: 1) A great many people with alcohol problems will refuse treatment if abstinence treatment (especially 12-step abstinence treatment) is all that's offered; 2) Many alcohol abusers can learn to drink moderately; and 3) Research has consistently shown that when offered a choice in goals, many who initially choose a moderation goal will switch to an abstinence goal after they fail to moderate. A great many of these individuals would choose to go untreated if their only option was, initially, abstinence-goal-only treatment. So, paradoxically, abstinence-only treatment might well *decrease* the number of alcohol abusers who achieve abstinence.

The concrete expression of this abstinence-goal-only treatment is the Minnesota Model. This 12-step Model makes no distinctions between alcohol abusers and alcohol-dependent persons, nor indeed between varying degrees of abuse or dependence. The prescription is the same for everyone: lifetime abstinence, whether the client is a teenager forced into treatment by parents after getting drunk once, or a 45-year-old chronic drinker suffering the DTs and liver damage.

Those who ask 12-step providers about moderating are routinely told that it's an impossibility for "alcoholics," that if they are alcoholic their "disease" will inevitably progress, that they should attempt to cut back, and that if they fail at that attempt (while being offered no help or support whatsoever—just insidious implications that they can't do it), they should come back for the only thing that works for alcoholics: abstinence treatment. The response of AA is about the same: problem drinkers are presumed to be alcoholic and are often told something to the effect of, "If you're wondering whether or not you belong here, you do." Those who ask about moderating are told that they are "in denial," that they should go out and try drinking moderately again (with the very strong implication that they can't do it), and that they should come back after they "hit bottom."

Researcher/writer William R. Miller notes:

> Another option, however, is to offer such clients the best available help in giving moderation a try. . . . The tone here, instead of "fail and come back" is more friendly: "if that's what you want, let's give it the best try we can, and see how it works." . . . An important element here is to [reassure] the client that, if the moderation experiment fails, you've given it the best try available, and then it would be time to consider abstinence.
>
> We have found that this can be effective in achieving abstinence with clients who are initially very resistant to the idea. A long-term (3.5-to-8-year) follow-up of 99 problem drinkers who tried a systemic moderation-oriented approach showed that more of them ultimately decided to abstain than maintain stable and problem-free moderation. It is noteworthy that of the abstainers in this study, more than half totally refused to consider abstinence

as an option before the trial, and of the remainder, most had said that they were willing to consider abstinence only if moderation failed. More than half of those who became long-term abstainers said, at follow-up, that the moderation trial had helped them recognize their need to abstain.[9]

Numerous other studies have confirmed these results.[10] It's also worthy of note that the massive Census Bureau-conducted study mentioned in Chapter 7, the National Longitudinal Alcoholism Epidemiological Survey, showed that of the formerly alcohol-dependent persons surveyed, at 20 or more years after the onset of dependence, 24% of the treated individuals were drinking without abuse or dependence, while fully 60% of the untreated individuals were drinking without abuse or dependence. (And, as mentioned previously, twice as many of the treated persons were still drinking abusively, 20% vs. 10%.)[11] These striking results provide good evidence that the "inevitable progressivity" of the disease concept is more myth than reality, that many alcohol abusers and outright "alcoholics" (alcohol dependent persons) do eventually "mature out" and learn to drink moderately, and that moderation-goal treatment should be a standard part of treatment options.

But there are very few such programs in North America. One of these is the low-cost program, DrinkWise. The inspiration for it came from psychologist Martha Sanchez-Craig. In the early 1970s, Sanchez-Craig began a career in the addictions treatment field by working at a halfway house in Toronto which operates in conjunction with the Addiction Research Foundation of Canada (ARF).

During her employment there, Sanchez-Craig became aware that some of the alcoholics in the halfway house had apparently learned to moderate their drinking and to reduce their alcohol consumption to two or three drinks per day. When word reached the management of the halfway house that Sanchez-Craig had discussed controlled drinking with one of the residents, she was accused of violating the total-abstinence philosophy of the establishment, and she was asked to resign. Only adamant support from the Addictions Research Foundation saved her job.

At the time, she was unsure of what these moderately drinking "alcoholics" implied in terms of alcoholism treatment; however, the situation provided a research opportunity, which she explored with the help of the ARF. She recruited 70 people who had come to the ARF for help, and she began a preliminary study. Twenty years of subsequent research have confirmed her initial findings.

Based on those findings, Sanchez-Craig and fellow researchers analyzed the behavior patterns surrounding alcohol use, and they devised a program to teach clients how to self-limit their alcohol intake. At follow-up interviews, approximately two-thirds of the clients reported staying within the guidelines and were not experiencing any health-related, legal, or employment difficulties.

DrinkWise

Largely through the efforts of Dr. Sanchez-Craig and the Addiction Research Foundation, the low-cost, commercial, early-intervention program DrinkWise began operations at Homewood Health Services in Guelph, Ontario in 1991. It began offering a consumer-ready program in the U.S. and Canada the following year. At present, DrinkWise has offices in Michigan and North Carolina.

DrinkWise is known as a "secondary prevention program" in that it is intended for individuals who already have mild to heavy drinking patterns. DrinkWise has a cognitive-behavioral base and is predicated upon the assumption that self-control comes through self-knowledge.

The first component of the program is screening. Individuals who currently are in a state of acute personal crisis, are chronically unemployed and lack social stability, are currently dependent upon illegal drugs, or have serious alcohol-related health problems are not accepted and are instead referred to other agencies. DrinkWise is intended for people who believe that they have the ability to manage their alcohol consumption or abstain, and who do not perceive themselves as "powerless" over alcohol.

The second component of the program is sobriety sampling. Clients are required to abstain from alcohol completely for the first two weeks of the program. This enables them to sample the experience of alcohol-free living, and it will uncover symptoms of withdrawal, if any.

The third component of the program is drink-counting. DrinkWise has ten moderate drinking guidelines:

1. No more than 12 drinks per week
2. No more than four drinks per day for men and three for women
3. No more than one drink per hour
4. No operation of any motorized vehicle while or after drinking
5. No drinking before or during work
6. No drinking before or while participating in sports or other physical activities
7. No drinking while pregnant or on prescription medication
8. No drinking with the intention of becoming intoxicated
9. No drinking to deal with depression, loneliness, or stress
10. No drinking out of habit

(These guidelines are quite conservative; the individuals in Sanchez-Craig's studies didn't begin to show evidence of alcohol-related problems until they were consuming at least 20 drinks per week.)

The final component of the DrinkWise program entails the use of a "drink diary." Clients are taught to note the number of their drinks, who they are with when they drink, where they drink, and how they feel when they drink or have the urge to do so. This allows clients to see their own drinking patterns, and so helps them make healthy changes in those patterns.

DrinkWise is not, however, alone. There are a number of free, non-12-step "alternative" self-help programs in the U.S. and Canada, including one moderation-goal program.

1. *The Natural History Alcoholism Revisited*, by George Vaillant. Cambridge, MA: Harvard University Press, 1995, pp. 254–269.
2. Ibid., p. 268.
3. "The Cost Effectiveness of Treatment for Alcoholism: A First Approximation," by H.D. Holder, et al. *Journal of Studies on Alcohol*, 1991, Volume 52, p. 52.
4. *Handbook of Alcoholism Treatment Approaches: Effective Alternatives*, Reid Hester and William Miller, eds. Boston: Allyn & Bacon, 1995.
5. Holder et al., op. cit., pp. 517–540.
6. "The Cost Effectiveness of Treatment for Alcoholism: A Second Approximation," by J.W. Finney and S.C. Monahan. *Journal of Studies on Alcohol*, 1996, Volume 57, pp. 229–242.
7. Hester and Miller, op. cit., p. 18.
8. *Resisting 12-Step Coercion: How to Fight Forced Participation in AA, NA, or 12-Step Treatment*, by Stanton Peele and Charles Bufe, with Archie Brodsky. Tucson, AZ: See Sharp Press, 2000, pp. 79–81.
9. "Warm Turkey," by William R. Miller and Andrew C. Page. *Journal of Substance Abuse Treatment*, Volume 8, 1991, pp. 227–232.
10. See Peele and Bufe, op. cit., pp. 74–77 for a discussion of these studies.
11. "Correlates of Past-Year Status Among Treated and Untreated Persons with Former Alcohol Dependence: United States, 1992," by Deborah Dawson. *Alcoholism: Clinical and Experimental Research*, Volume 20, 1996, pp. 771–779.

10

Alternative Self-Help Groups

Since the establishment of Alcoholics Anonymous as an independent organization in 1939, there have been a number of attempts to found "alternative" addictions self-help groups. Some of these, such as Jewish Alcoholics and Chemically Dependent and Significant Others (JACS) and the Calix Society, can be considered as mere adjuncts to AA, in that they support AA and its ideology, and in that they expect their members to attend AA. Another self-help group, Alcoholics Victorious (AV), is a specifically Christian adaptation of the AA program. AV mentions, for example, "Jesus Christ," rather than AA's deliberately euphemistic "Power greater than ourselves," in its steps.

But what of true, nonreligious alternatives to AA? There have been a number of attempts to establish such programs. One relatively early example is the work of Bill Talley in Denver, Colorado. In the early 1980s, Talley began his attempts to establish alternative self-help groups. He used several names, such as Turning Points in Sobriety, Methods of Moderation and Abstinence, and American Atheists Addiction Recovery Groups. All of these made use of psychologist Albert Ellis's rational-emotive behavior therapy, a usage which presaged its use in two later "alternative" self-help groups (Rational Recovery and SMART Recovery). Talley's support groups never spread beyond Denver, although he did publish newsletters which spread his message nationally. Talley ceased his efforts in the early 1990s and died shortly thereafter. His attempts to establish alternative, nonreligious self-help groups died with him.

There have, however, been a number of successful attempts to establish nonreligious addictions self-help groups. The longest-surviving such group is Women for Sobriety.

Women for Sobriety

Women for Sobriety (WFS) was founded by sociologist Jean Kirk-patrick in 1976. She did this in large part because from their very beginnings AA and 12-step treatment have been heavily male dominated. This can be traced all the way back to the two co-founders of AA, and the exclusively male make-up of AA for its first several years. The bias in 12-step treatment can be traced back to the AA questionnaire analyzed by E.M. Jellinek, which provided the basis of his book, *The Disease Concept of Alcoholism*, and his two articles in the *Quarterly Journal of Studies on Alcohol*. The responses of men and women to the questionnaire varied radically. Jellinek writes, "[T]he data differed so greatly for the two sexes that merging the data was inadvisable."[1] This is important in that Jellinek's work provides much of the "scientific" basis for 12-step treatment, and in that this basis was provided exclusively by male respondents. Although the recovery needs of women apparently differ significantly from those of men, both AA and 12-step treatment provide a one-size-fits-all approach for both women and men. WFS was designed to deal with this obvious flaw.

Women for Sobriety differs significantly in other ways from AA. For one, WFS is nonreligious (although it is an abstinence program). Its New Life Program is encapsulated in its Thirteen Statements of Acceptance:

1. I have a drinking (life-threatening) problem that once had me. We now take charge of our life and our disease. We accept the responsibility.
2. Negative thoughts destroy only myself. Our first conscious sober act must be to remove negativity from our life.
3. Happiness is a habit I will develop. Happiness is created, not waited for.
4. Problems bother me only to the degree I permit them to. We now better understand our problems and do not permit problems to overwhelm us.
5. I am what I think. I am a capable, competent, caring, compassionate woman.
6. Life can be ordinary or it can be great. Greatness is mine by a conscious effort.
7. Love can change the course of my world. Caring becomes all important.
8. The fundamental object of life is emotional and spiritual growth. Daily I put my life into a proper order, knowing which are the priorities.
9. The past is gone forever. No longer will I be victimized by the past. I am a new person.
10. All love given returns. I will learn to know that others love me.

11. Enthusiasm is my daily exercise. I treasure all moments of my new life.
12. I am a competent woman and have much to give life. This is what I am and I shall know it always.
13. I am responsible for myself and for my actions. I am in charge of my mind, my thoughts, and my life.

When presented in the form of levels for recovery, the WFS Program is thus:

Level I: Accepting Alcoholism as a physical disease.
"I have a drinking (life-threatening) problem that once had me." (#1)

Level II: Discarding negative thoughts, putting guilt behind, and practicing new ways of viewing and solving problems.
"Negative thoughts destroy only myself." (#2)
"Problems bother me only to the degree I permit them to." (#4)
"The past is gone forever." (#9)

Level III: Creating and practicing a new self-image.
"I am what I think." (#5)
"I am a competent woman and have much to give to life." (#12)

Level IV: Using new attitudes to enforce new behavior patterns.
"Happiness is a habit I will develop." (#3)
"Life can be ordinary or it can be great." (#6)
"Enthusiasm is my daily exercise." (#11)

Level V: Improving relationships as a result of our new feelings about self.
"Love can change the course of my world." (#7)
"All love given returns." (#10)

Level VI: Recognizing life's priorities: emotional and spiritual growth, self-responsibility.
"The fundamental object of life is emotional and spiritual growth." (#8)
"I am responsible for myself and my actions." (#13)

Women for Sobriety's program is spelled out in more detail in founder Kirkpatrick's books, *Turnabout: Help for a New Life* and *Goodbye Hangovers, Hello Life*.

WFS has self-help groups, primarily in the U.S., but also in Canada, Europe, Australia, and New Zealand.

Contact Information:

Women for Sobriety
P.O. Box 618
Quakertown, PA 18951
Telephone: 215-536-8026 / 800-333-1605
E-mail: WFSobriety@aol.com
Web Site: www.womenforsobriety.org

Secular Organizations for Sobriety (SOS)

Secular Organizations for Sobriety was founded by James Christopher in 1986. It is a nonprofit, abstinence-oriented secular alternative to AA, and is affiliated with the Council for Secular Humanism (formerly Council for Democratic and Secular Humanism). SOS has as its centerpiece its Sobriety Priority program, which employs the use of "Cognitive/Visceral Synchronization" and principles of cognitive therapy. SOS views addictions as having three major components: a physiological need; a learned habit; and a denial of the need and habit.

SOS's program is distilled in its Suggested Guidelines for Sobriety:

1. To break the cycle of denial and achieve sobriety, we must first acknowledge that we are alcoholics or addicts.
2. We reaffirm this truth daily and accept without reservation that, as clean and sober individuals, we can not and do not drink or use, no matter what.
3. Since drinking or using is not an option for us, we take whatever steps are necessary to continue our Sobriety Priority lifelong.
4. A quality of life—"the good life"—can be achieved. However, life is also filled with uncertainties. Therefore, we do not drink or use regardless of feelings, circumstances or conflicts.
5. We share in confidence with each other and our thoughts and feelings as sober, clear individuals.
6. Sobriety is our priority, and we are each responsible for our lives and our sobriety.

The SOS program is spelled out in more detail in founder Christopher's books, *How to Stay Sober: Recovery Without Religion, Unhooked: Staying Sober and Drug Free*, and *Sobriety Handbook: The SOS Way*. SOS maintains a network of support groups in 28 U.S. states, Canada, Iceland, France, England, and Belgium.

Contact Information:

Secular Organizations for Sobriety
5521 Grosvenor Blvd.
Los Angeles, CA 90066
Telephone: 310-821-8430
E-mail: sosa@loop.com
Web sites: www.unhooked.com /

Rational Recovery (RR)

Rational Recovery was founded in 1986 by Jack and Lois Trimpey, and was originally based in part on Albert Ellis's rational-emotive behavior therapy (REBT). RR grew rapidly during its first few years, and by the early 1990s had perhaps 800 to 1000 support groups in the U.S., making it the largest nonreligious addictions self-help organization ever to exist in the United States. But at about that time RR's founders abandoned REBT (declaring it useless as a means of combating addictions) in favor of what they call "planned abstinence" through the use of their registered Addictive Voice Recognition Technique® (AVRT®). They have subsequently declared self-help groups of all types worse than useless in dealing with addictions, and at the turn of the millennium ordered all remaining RR self-help groups to disband.

Rational Recovery explains its technique as follows:

AVRT® Quick Start

- Chemical dependence is simply the use of a substance for its effect.
- Addiction is chemical dependency against your own better judgment.
- Addicted people are of two minds about the use of the substance. To drink/use or not to drink/use: ah, yes—that is the question!
- Be honest with yourself. You drink/use for the pleasurable effect of the drug. We call the desire for the effect of alcohol, The Beast.
- The Beast of RR can talk in your thoughts, and it has feelings. It wants to survive.
- The Addictive Voice (AV) is any thinking that supports or suggests the possible future use of alcohol or drugs.
- The sole cause of your addiction is the AV.
- The disease concept is a perfect example of the AV.
- Recovery groups and addiction treatment are pure AV.
- When you recognize your AV it can no longer control you., i.e., "It" wants to drink/use, but "I" don/t.

- No one is ever "out of control," although addicted people frequently change their minds and make poor judgments.
- The worst way to quit something you love is one-day-at-a-time.
- The best way to quit your addiction is once, for all time.

Those interested in more information on RR and its Addictive Voice Recognition Technique® can find it on RR's web site (see below) or in Jack Trimpey's *The Final Fix for Alcohol and Drug Addiction: AVRT* and *Rational Recovery: The New Cure for Substance Addiction*. RR also maintains a number of Rational Recovery Centers where AVRT® is taught.

Contact Information:

Rational Recovery Systems, Inc.
P.O. Box 800
Lotus, CA 95651
Telephone: 530-621-4374 / 800-303-CURE
E-mail: rr@rational.org
Web Site: www.rational.org

Self Management and Recovery Training
(SMART or SMART Recovery)

When Rational Recovery's president, Jack Trimpey, abandoned rational-emotive behavior therapy (REBT), RR consisted of two corporations: a for-profit and a nonprofit (which had incorporated in 1992). A large majority of the board of directors of the nonprofit corporation —which was responsible for overseeing the self-help group aspect of RR—were professional rational-emotive behavior therapists. Following Trimpey's abandonment of REBT, the nonprofit corporation began operating as SMART Recovery in 1994.

The emphasis in SMART groups is on the identification and elimination (or alteration) of self-destructive attitudes and behaviors. SMART is based on the belief that unless such patterns are successfully identified and dealt with, individuals may repeat them—as in the case of "relapse." To identify and deal with unhealthy patterns—especially those related to addictions— SMART utilizes the principles and methods of REBT. SMART also rejects the "one day at a time approach," and instead encourages its members to adopt long-range life goals and to implement short-range strategies to achieve those goals.

The SMART program has three primary aims. The first is abstinence from alcohol. The second is to nurture emotional independence and self-reliance. And the third is to assist individuals in giving up dependence upon support groups. This last aim is predicated on the view that emotional dependence upon anything, including support groups, tends to be unhealthy. It is also predicated upon the belief that positive therapeutic change is almost always accomplished in a limited amount of time.

SMART Recovery Purposes and Methods

1. We help individuals gain independence from addictive behavior.
2. We teach how to:
   A. Enhance and maintain motivation to abstain.
   B. Cope with urges.
   C. Manage thoughts, feelings and behavior.
   D. Balance momentary and enduring satisfactions.
3. Our efforts are based on scientific knowledge, and evolve as scientific knowledge evolves.
4. Individuals who have gained independence from addiction are invited to stay involved with us, to enhance their gains and help others.

At present, SMART has several hundred meetings across the U.S. in 34 states, as well as meetings in Canada, Australia, Scotland, and Sweden. The two self-help books most commonly used in SMART are, probably, *When AA Doesn't Work for You*, by Albert Ellis and Emmett Velten, and *Alcohol: How to Give It Up and Be Glad You Did*, by Philip Tate.

Contact Information:

SMART Recovery
7537 Mentor Ave. #306
Mentor, OH 44060
Telephone: 440-951-5357
Fax: 440-951-5358
E-mail: Srmail@aol.com
Web Site: www.smartrecovery.org

Moderation Management (MM)

Moderation Management was founded by Audrey Kishline in 1993. It is the only one of the "alternative" self-help groups dedicated to helping problem drinkers moderate their drinking, rather than abstain. Like those of the other "alternative" self-help groups, MM's meetings are free. The two basic requirements for MM membership are a willingness to take responsibility for one's actions and behaviors, and a desire to moderate the consumption of alcoholic beverages.

MM's approach is very cautious and bears striking similarities to the DrinkWise program mentioned in the previous chapter. MM emphasizes that its program is intended for those with relatively mild alcohol problems, and refers those with more serious problems to abstinence-goal groups. As well, MM's guidelines for moderate drinking are also very much on the cautious, conservative side. Like DrinkWise, MM is predicated on the belief that an ounce of prevention is worth a pound of cure.

The only ways in which MM is similar to AA are that it's a free self-help group and that it has a set of steps (totally different, however, from AA's):

MM's Nine Steps Toward Moderation

1. Attend meetings and learn about the program Moderation Management.
2. Abstain from alcoholic beverages for 30 days and complete steps three through six during this time.
3. Examine how drinking has affected your life.
4. Write down your priorities.
5. Take a look at how much, how often, and under what circumstances you used to drink.
6. Learn MM guidelines for moderate drinking.
7. Set moderate drinking limits and start weekly "small steps" toward positive lifestyle changes.
8. Review your progress at meetings and update your goals.
9. After achieving your goal of moderation, attend MM meetings any time you feel the need for support, or would like to help newcomers.

Moderation Management Limits

1. Never drive while impaired by the effects of alcohol.
2. Do not drink in situations that would endanger yourself or others.
3. Do not drink every day. MM suggests that you do not drink more than 3 or 4 days per week.
4. For women: Do not drink more than 3 drinks on any day, and no more than 9 drinks per week.
5. For men: Do not drink more than 4 drinks on any day, and no more than 14 drinks per week.

For further details on the MM program, see *Moderate Drinking: The Moderation Management Guide*, by Audrey Kishline. MM currently has meetings in 15 U.S. states and Canada, as well as active on-line meetings.

Contact Information:

Moderation Management
P.O. Box 3055
Point Pleasant NJ 08742
Telephone: 1-732-295-0949
E-mail: moderation@moderation.org
Web Site: www.moderation.org

A Note on the Kishline Tragedy: In March 2000, MM founder Audrey Kishline, while blind drunk, drove her pickup truck down the wrong side of a freeway in Washington state, ran head on into another vehicle, and killed a father and his 12-year-old daughter. Following this tragedy, there were numerous denunciations in the press of the moderation-goal approach to alcoholism treatment. Curiously, almost none of these denunciations mentioned that Kishline had spent years in AA prior to founding MM and that she had undergone a 28-day, 12-step inpatient treatment program. And almost none of the denunciations mentioned that in January 2000, two months prior to the crash, Kishline had publicly announced on the MM e-mail list that she was having difficulties maintaining moderation and was instead returning to an abstinence goal and AA.

One of the denunciations of moderation goals (which was picked up widely in the press) was issued by Stacia Murphy, president of the 12-step front group, National Council on Alcoholism and Drug Dependence. In an NCADD press release, Murphy vigorously denounced moderation-goal treatment, but made no mention of Kishline's prior AA involvement, her 12-step inpatient treatment, or that she had abandoned MM and was attending AA at the time of the crash. When asked why she had not mentioned Kishline's extensive AA involvement, Murphy replied that she thought it "irrelevant."

---

1. "Phases in the Drinking of Alcoholics: Analysis of a Survey Conducted by the Official Organ of Alcoholics Anonymous," by E.M. Jellinek. *Quarterly Journal of Studies on Alcohol*, Vol. 7 No. 1, 1946, p. 6.

11

Conclusions and Recommendations

No other area of American commerce and human interaction is more sadly lacking, in terms of adequate consumer information and protection, than the mental health field. This is, in large measure, due to the qualitative nature of most therapeutic approaches. The subjective nature of psychotherapy, family therapy, individual psychological counseling, and addictions counseling/therapy makes an accurate quantitative analysis of treatment outcomes difficult. In addition, the short-term nature of most clinical studies, and their lack of control groups, further distorts the nature and scope of clinical findings. Uncontrolled studies very often produce the illusion of positive treatment outcomes when exactly the opposite is probably the case.

Ironically enough, the one area within the mental health field in which a reasonably accurate long-term methodological analysis of treatment outcomes is possible, and has in fact been successfully undertaken—and where adequate consumer information and consumer protection would be most expected—is the very area in which consumer protection and information is *least* available to the public. That area is, of course, addictions treatment.

Despite the fact that the best available research evidence has consistently indicated that the Minnesota Model, its components, and other 12-step approaches lack efficacy, the public is almost entirely unaware of this, and these ineffective treatments continue to be the norm. The result is that by far the most common treatment outcome for alcoholics and addicts receiving professional addictions treatment, counseling, and therapy is *relapse*. The relapse rate for treated alcoholics and addicts is remarkably high and remarkably consistent.

Although 12-step treatment centers typically tout recovery rates as high as 70%, 80%, 90%, or even 95%, they arrive at these statistics through highly dubious methods. To claim such high recovery rates, they routinely ignore treatment dropouts (normally high in 12-step treatment), ignore clients they have been unable to track after release (many of whom have likely relapsed), and they use short-term outcome measures—and all this without the use of control or comparison groups. To better appreciate the fudging of these statistics, realize that one-year studies are considered to be "long term" in the addictions field, and that significant relapse often occurs in the one-to-five-year period after treatment. To further appreciate the dubious nature of these statistics, consider that the two best truly long-term studies of treated and untreated alcoholics (the Vaillant and NLAES studies) both indicate that treated alcoholics fare no better than untreated alcoholics; and the NLAES indicates that untreated alcoholics tend to fare *better* in the long run (20+ years after the onset of dependence) than those who have undergone treatment.

In their *Handbook of Alcoholism Treatment Approaches*, William Miller and Reid Hester comment on the inefficacy of standard treatment approaches:

> The negative correlation between scientific evidence and application in standard [addictions treatment] practice remains striking and could hardly be larger if one intentionally constructed treatment programs with the *least* evidence of effectiveness.[1]

They go on to plead that clinicians in the alcoholism/addictions treatment field set aside their cherished preconceptions and instead rely on scientific evidence in formulating and applying methods of treatment. They cite the following commentary from a very different field (biblical historicity scholarship), suggesting that the reader substitute the word "clinician" for "scholar":

> To be a critical scholar means to make empirical, factual evidence—evidence open to confirmation by independent neutral observers—the controlling factor in [professional] judgements. Noncritical scholars are those who put dogmatic considerations first and insist that factual evidence confirm [their] premises. Critical scholars adopt the principle of methodological skepticism: accept only what passes the rigorous test of the rules of evidence.[2]

That statement was cited by Miller and Hester in 1995; very little has changed in the addictions field in the following years. The relatively small movement toward implementing effective treatment approaches has been propelled almost entirely by clinicians outside of the 12-step mainstream, while those in the mainstream have remained fixated upon treatment approaches with negative evidence of efficacy: AA; 12-step inpatient treatment; psychotherapy; general alcoholism counseling (by paraprofessionals); educational lectures and films; and confrontational counseling. In fact, as the Kishline affair (see p. 137) well demonstrates, those in the 12-step mainstream are not only extremely attached to their ineffective methods, but a great many of them are actively hostile to approaches with better evidence of efficacy, and will stoop to outright misrepresentation in their efforts to thwart them.

As we saw in Chapter 8, there are reasons for this. The primary one is that addictions professionals in this country come primarily from the ranks of the formerly addicted. They became 12-step true believers while in treatment; they were then recruited into the profession by other 12-step true believers (their counselors); and they in turn recruit yet more true believers from the ranks of those they treat. In many ways, addictions treatment in the United States is a closed, incestuous profession. One of the primary results of the closed, incestuous nature of U.S. addiction treatment is the "groupthink" phenomenon. Joseph C. Kern, former director of addictions treatment services in Nassau County, New York describes it as follows:

> Janis (1982) has shown how the Gestalt of a working group can have a dramatic impact on product outcomes. He has identified several aspects of a phenomenon called "groupthink," which is characterized by a single-minded rigidity of purpose which defies corrective feedback, a closed information system, [which is] demanding of loyalty and [the avoidance of] internal and external criticism, and [which produces a system] which only adds new members who will conform to the existing belief system and norms of the group. This phenomenon can have a devastating, negative impact on decision making, since the group avoids new information and contact with reality. Hence their decisions become less appropriate to problem-solving and more interested in preserving the group's norms and belief system.[3]

This is exactly the situation in the addictions treatment field. The staffs of most treatment centers believe religiously (and often unanimously) in the 12-step approach, and the overwhelming number of clients are forced to endure the same simplistic religious program that virtually all of the treatment staff adhere to. Clients are simply forced into accepting the 12-steps within treatment centers, and because of the cult-like nature of 12-step treatment are usually entirely unaware that effective alternative treatments exist. (Twelve-step treatment centers routinely refuse to allow clients access to any reading matter other than approved, 12-step "recovery" materials.)

Many clients then relapse and are again forced through the same type of 12-step treatment; and again they're denied information about effective alternatives. This cycle can, and does, repeat itself over and over, with a great many clients going through treatment, relapsing, and then being re-treated as many as 10, 15, even 20 or 25 times. In no other field of medicine would this be tolerated. In any other field, treatments shown to lack efficacy would not be employed. And any treatment that failed to produce betterment in a patient would be quickly abandoned in favor of alternative treatments—especially if those alternatives had better evidence of efficacy than the original treatment.

But in addictions treatment the repeated application of ineffective treatment modalities is the norm. There is an additional reason for this beyond the religious zeal of 12-step treatment providers: AA/12-step ideology places the blame for treatment failures on *clients*, not treatment providers. This attitude is summed up by the AA slogan, "It works if you work it." In other words, the program is perfect and if the client relapses it's entirely his or her own fault. In fact, when relapse does occur, the only options 12-step therapists will normally offer their clients is advice such as, "Go to more meetings" or "Go back into treatment." In AA, when relapse occurs, the fault is *never* AA's, and the AA members in the relapser's "home group" will often speculate about what the relapser did "wrong," wondering, for instance, whether he "left something out" of his fifth step.

So, the 12-step approach serves 12-step treatment providers very well: it provides a simplistic, one-size-fits-all approach that even those with essentially no medical or psychological training can (and do) easily apply; and it supplies them with the perfect excuse for treatment failures—the fault is *always* the client's, not the treatment provider's nor the treatment modality's. In the end, 12-step treatment providers hold up their relatively few successes as "proof" that "it works if you work it," while, para-doxically, the many, many treatment failures also supply "proof" that 12-step treatment "works"—they provide "proof" of what happens if you don't "work a good program" or lack "honesty."

Given all this, it's entirely unrealistic to expect that any kind of reform will come from within the ranks of 12-step treatment providers. They are, to be blunt, close-minded religious folk much like religious funda-mentalists opposed to evolution. In order to maintain their sacred beliefs, both groups ignore the best available scientific evidence while inventing bogus statistics (in the case of fundamentalists, bogus "evidence") and grasping at any straw, no matter how flimsy, that seems to lend support to their dogmatic beliefs. As with fundamentalists, 12-step true believers place belief before evidence: they discard all evidence (no matter how strong) that calls their sacred beliefs into question, and fashion what's left into support for their beliefs. This is the exact opposite of standard scientific practice in which hypotheses, theories, and laws flow *from* evaluation of *all* available evidence.

What's To Be Done?

There are a number of long-term solutions to this dismal situation. These include such things as requiring that addictions counselors undergo several years of training in scientific, medical, and/or psychological disciplines in academic institutions, that addictions treatment facilities be forced to open their records to independent researchers, and that the results of their studies be made available to the public via consumer protection agencies. Given the political climate in this country, however, other more immediate approaches are also needed.

There are a number that can, and to a varying degree *are*, being implemented by individuals and institutions. A few of them follow:

1. *Legal action against treatment providers.*
   A. Approximately 2,000,000 Americans go through formal alcoholism/ addictions treatment every year, and more than half of them are forced to do so. Probably at least half of the coerced individuals are neither alcoholics nor addicts. While a large majority of such individuals are in no position to sue because of lack of economic resources and/or threats of job loss, professional decertification, denial of parole, or revocation of probation or parole, a small number of coerced individuals *are* in a position to sue, and some of them win when they sue. For example, in May 1999 Dr. Leonard Masters won a suit against former (1997–1999) ASAM President and prominent 12-step treatment provider and advocate, Dr. G. Douglas Talbott, and two of his associates, for deliberate misdiagnosis, breach of fiduciary duty, and false imprisonment. Masters received $1.3 million as compensatory damages and an undisclosed amount in punitive damages.[4]
   B. Individuals coerced into 12-step treatment by government agencies can challenge such coercion on the grounds that AA, NA, and 12-step treatment are religious in nature, and therefore such mandates violate the Establishment Clause of the First Amendment. There have been a number of such cases in recent years, and plaintiffs (that is, those suing the government agencies) have won all four cases which have reached the appeals level. Two of those cases were decided by state high courts (Evans v. Tennessee Board of Paroles, 1997, and Warner v. Orange County [NY] Department of Probation, 1999), and two by federal appeals courts (Kerr v. Farrey, 1996, and Griffin v. Coughlin, 1996).
   Again, for the reasons mentioned above, most persons coerced by government agencies into 12-step attendance will be in no position to sue. As well, in 2000 the Supreme Court refused to consider the Griffin case, so there is as yet no national binding precedent on this issue. But in the

absence of binding precedents, courts tend to rely on precedents established by appeals courts, and the existing decisions have stated unequivocally that AA, NA, and 12-step treatment are religious in nature, so anyone pressing a case against a government agency on Establishment Clause grounds would stand a very good chance of winning, eventually.[5]

2. *Press government agencies to fund only addictions treatment programs utilizing treatment modalities with good evidence of efficacy.* Admittedly, this will not likely result in immediate change, but it could pay dividends in the long run. There are a number of ways of doing this. Probably the most effective is to contact public officials directly and to agitate via letters to the editor, op-ed pieces, and the Internet.

3. *Press insurers to fund only addictions treatment programs utilizing treatment modalities with good evidence of efficacy.* This approach will probably yield more immediate results, as private insurers have an additional motivation largely absent from government agencies—the desire to save money. Those outside the insurance industry can probably pursue this most effectively through the media by pointing out the lack of efficacy of common (12-step) treatment methods and their high cost. Again, the best avenues for doing this are probably letters to the editor, op-ed pieces, and the Internet.

Those in the insurance industry—especially executives and "bean counters"—can take a more direct approach. Indeed, there already have been promising moves motivated by cost-saving. Insurers have drastically reduced funding for 12-step inpatient treatment through reduced eligibility criteria, through reducing the number of inpatient treatment episodes for which insurees are eligible (or eliminating inpatient eligibility altogether), and through reducing the number of days of treatment per treatment episode for which they'll pay. In the gravy-train years of the mid 1980s, insurers commonly paid for a full 28 days of treatment, with insurees eligible for repeated treatment episodes. Nowadays, insurers (if they'll pay for inpatient treatment at all) commonly will pay for only one to three treatment episodes, and for only five to seven days per treatment episode.

If insurers were to go entirely by the best available scientific evidence, they'd save a bundle. They'd entirely stop paying for 12-step treatment and would pay only for low-cost, short-term, cognitive-behavioral approaches such as brief intervention and motivational enhancement. One can only hope that the very persuasive scientific evidence and their own financial self-interest will lead them to do this sooner rather than later. And a few nudges in that direction in the media and by those inside the industry certainly can't hurt.

4. *Press the media to do its job.* Journalists tend to be overworked and, often, lazy. Thus one sees puff piece after puff piece on AA and 12-step treatment, in which journalists accept at face value the self-serving statements and cooked statistics provided by AA members, AA front groups such as the NCADD and ASAM, and 12-step treatment providers. If such a piece appears in your local media, approach the reporter(s) respectfully and ask them if they're aware that their piece contains inaccuracies. In some cases they'll respond positively, in others (especially where they're simply lazy) they'll blow you off, and in others they'll be actively hostile (especially if they're 12-steppers hiding behind "anonymity" while they promote AA). In the latter two cases, complain to their editors about inaccuracies in their stories. There's always a chance that a corrective piece will appear, or you might be invited to write an op-ed piece.

While none of this will lead to immediate progressive change in the treatment of addictions, cumulatively it will have an effect. The current addictions treatment system is religiously (not scientifically) based, coercive, ineffective, and expensive, and it cannot hide those faults forever —no matter how slick its propaganda machine and no matter how many friends (and hidden 12-step members) it has in the media. In the end the truth will prevail, and there will be a drastic overhaul of the treatment of addictions in this country.

The question is when.

---

1. *Handbook of Alcoholism Treatment Approaches: Effective Alternatives (Second Edition)*, Reid Hester and William Miller, eds. Boston: Allyn & Bacon, 1995, p. 33.
2. *The Five Gospels: The Search for the Authentic Words of Jesus*, by R.W. Funk, R.W. Hoover, and The Jesus Seminar. New York: MacMillan, 1993, p. 34.
3. "The Dysfunctional Alcoholism Agency" (taped lecture), by Joseph C. Kern at the Northeast Regional Conference of the National Association for Children of Alcoholics, November 14–15, 1986.
4. See *Resisting 12-Step Coercion: How to Fight Forced Participation in AA, NA, or 12-Step Treatment*, by Stanton Peele, Charles Bufe, and Archie Brodsky. Tucson, AZ: See Sharp Press, 2000, Chapter 6, pp. 143–153.
5. Ibid., chapters 3 and 4, pp. 82–129.

Bibliography

Anonymous (no author listed)
—*Al-Anon Spoken Here.* New York: Al-Anon Family Group Headquarters, 1984.
—*Dr. Bob and the Good Oldtimers.* New York: Alcoholics Anonymous World Services, 1980.
—*Pass It On.* New York: Alcoholics Anonymous World Services, 1984.
—*The A.A. Service Manual.* New York: Alcoholics Anonymous World Services, 1989.
—*For 50 Years, The Voice of Americans Fighting Alcoholism.*
   http://www.ncadd.org/50yrs.html
—*Narcotics Anonymous: A Commitment to Community Partnerships.*
   http://www.wsoinc.com/sandiego.htm
—*The Progression and Recovery of the Alcoholic.* Parkside Medical Corp., 1988.
—*The Treatment Episode Data Set (TEDS): 1992–1997, National Admissions to Substance Abuse Treatment.* Rock Springs, MD: Substance Abuse and Mental Health Services Administration, 1999.
Abbot, Stephanie. *The National Association for Children of Alcoholics Newsletter*, Volume 10, September/October 1994.
Ackerman, Robert. *Growing in the Shadow.* Pompano Beach, FL: Health Communications, 1986.
Behr, Edward. *Prohibition: Thirteen Years that Changed America.* New York: Arcade Publishing, 1996.
Blocker, Jack S. *American Temperance Movements: Cycles of Reform.* Boston, MA: K.G. Hall & Co., 1989.
Bowden, Julie and Gravits, Herbert. *Recovery: A Guide for Adult Children of Alcoholics.* New York: Simon and Schuster, 1987.
Braden, Charles S. *These Also Believe: A Study of Modern Cults and Minority Religious Movements.* New York: Macmillan, 1949.
Bufe, Charles. *Alcoholics Anonymous: Cult or Cure? (Second Edition).* Tucson, AZ: See Sharp Press, 1998.
Cain, Arthur. "Alcoholics Anonymous: Cult or Cure?" *Harper's*, February 1963, pp. 48–52.
—"Alcoholics Can Be Cured—Despite A.A." *Saturday Evening Post*, September 19, 1965, pp. 6–8.
Chiauzzi, Emil J. and Liljgren, Steven. "Taboo Topics in Addiction Treatment." *Journal of Substance Abuse Treatment*, Volume 10, 1993, pp. 303–316.
Clifford, Mark. "Selling Synanon." *Forbes*, Volume 137 Number 12, June 2, 1986.
Dawson, Deborah. "Correlates of Past-Year Status Among Treated and Untreated Persons with Former Alcohol Dependence: United States, 1992." *Alcoholicsm: Clinical and Experimental Research*, Volume 20, 1996, pp. 771–779.
Ditman, Keith. "A Controlled Experiment on the Use of Court Probation for Drunk Arrests." *American Journal of Psychiatry*, August 1967, pp. 64–67.
Driberg, Tom. *The Mystery of Moral Re-Armament.* New York: Alfred A. Knopf, 1965.
Emrick, Chad. "A Review of Psychologically Oriented Treatment of Alcoholism." *Journal of Studies on Alcohol*, Volume 36, 1975, pp. 88–108.

Fingarette, Herbert. *Heavy Drinking: The Myth of Alcoholism as a Disease.* Berkeley, CA: University of California Press, 1988.

Finney, John and Moos, Rudolf. "The Long-Term Course of Treated Alcoholism: I. Mortality, Relapse, Remission Rates and Community Controls." *Journal of Studies on Alcohol,* Volume 52 Number 1, 1991, pp. 44–54.

—"The Cost Effectiveness of Treatment for Alcoholism: A Second Approximation." *Journal of Studies on Alcohol,* 1996, Volume 57, pp. 229–242.

Fitzgerald, Kathleen W. *Alcoholism: The Genetic Inheritance.* New York: Doubleday, 1988.

Floyd, Anthony. "Alcoholism Outcome Studies." *Addictive Behaviors,* July/August 1996.

Fox, Vince. *Addiction, Change and Choice: The New View of Alcoholism.* Tucson, AZ: See Sharp Press, 1993.

Funk, R.W. and Hover, R.W. *The Five Gospels: The Search for the Authentic Words of Jesus.* New York: Macmillan, 1993.

Gerard, Donald, Saenger, Gerhardt, and Wile Renee. "The Abstinent Alcoholic." *Archives of General Psychiatry,* Volume 6, 1982.

Gerstel, David. *Paradise Incorporated: Synanon.* Novato, CA: Presidio Press, 1982.

Gorski, Terence. "Penny Wise, Pound Foolish." *Addiction and Recovery Newsletter,* May/June 1992.

—"Chemical Dependency and Mental Health: Avoiding a Shotgun Merger." *Behavioral Health Management,* January 1994.

Gorski Terence and Marlatt, Alan. "Alcoholism: Disease or Addiction?" *Professional Counselor,* October 1996.

Graham, James. *Vessels of Rage, Engines of Power.* Lexington, VA: Aculeus Press, 1994.

Hester, Reid K. and Miller, William R. (eds.). *Handbook of Alcoholism Treatment Approaches: Effective Alternatives (Second Edition).* Boston: Allyn & Bacon, 1995.

Holder, H.D., et al. "The Cost Effectiveness of Treatment for Alcoholism: A First Approximation." *Journal of Studies on Alcohol,* 1991, Volume 52, pp. 517–540.

Howard, Peter. *Britain and the Beast.* London: Heinemann, 1963.

Jellinek, Elvin M. *The Disease Concept of Alcoholism.* Piscataway, NJ: Alcohol Research Documentation, 1960.

Kern, Joseph C. "The Dysfunctional Alcoholism Agency" (lecture, audio cassette). National Association for Children of Alcoholics, Northeast Regional Conference, November 14–15, 1986.

Larsen, Joan M. *Alcoholism: The Biochemical Connection.* New York: Random House, 1992.

Lean, Garth. *On the Tail of a Comet.* Colorado Springs, CO: Helms and Howard, 1988.

Miller, William R. and Meyers, Robert J. "Beyond Genetic Criteria: Reflections on Life After Clinical Science Wins." *Clinical Science,* Spring 1995, pp. 2–6.

Miller, William R. and Page, Andrew C. "Warm Turkey." *Journal of Substance Abuse Treatment,* Volume 8, 1991.

Mitchell, David and Kathy, and Ofshe, Richard. *The Light on Synanon.* New York: Seaview Books, 1980.

Nobleman, Susan. "COA's working in the Alcoholism Field: A Return to the Family of Origin" (lecture, audio cassette). National Association for Children of Alcoholics, Northeast Regional Conference, November 14–15, 1986.

Peele, Stanton. *Diseasing of America.* Lexington, MA: Lexington Books, 1989.

Peele, Stanton, Bufe, Charles, and Brodsky, Archie. *Resisting 12-Step Coercion: How to Fight Forced Participation in AA, NA, or 12-Step Treatment.* Tucson, AZ: See Sharp Press, 2000.

Pell, Sidney and D'Alanzo, C.A. "A Five Year Study of Alcoholics." *Journal of Occupational Medicine*, February 1973, pp. 120–125.

Plaut, Thomas (ed.). *Alcohol Problems: A Report to the Nation.* New York: Oxford University Press, 1967.

Polich, Michael J., et al. *The Course of Alcoholism Four Years After Treatment.* New York: John Wiley and Sons, 1980.

Powell, Barbara, et al. "Comparison of Three Outpatient Interventions: A Twelve Month Follow-Up of Male Alcoholics." *Journal of Studies on Alcohol*, Volume 46, 1985.

Radner, Nancy W. "The Last Word." *The Humanist*, September/October 1997, p. 2.

Ragge, Ken. *The Real AA: Behind the Myth of 12-Step Recovery.* Tucson, AZ: See Sharp Press, 1998.

Robertson, Nan. *Getting Better Inside Alcoholics Anonymous.* New York: William Morrow, 1988.

Room, Robin. "Healing Ourselves and Our Planet." *Contemporary Drug Problems*, Volume 9, 1992, pp. 717–740.

Severan, William. *The End of the Roaring Twenties: Prohibition and Repeal.* New York: Simon and Schuster, 1969.

Tally, William. "Secular Heresy: Should Peer Support End?" *Recovery*, June/July 1984.

Timberlake, James. *Prohibition and the Progressive Movement, 1900–1920.* Boston, MA: Harvard University Press, 1963.

Vaillant, George. *The Natural History of Alcoholism Revisited.* Cambridge, MA: Harvard University Press, 1995.

Walter, Robin R. "Codependence? Nonsense." *RN*, Volume 58, February 1995.

Wegscheider-Cruse, Sharon. *Choice Making.* Pompano Beach, FL: Health Communications, 1985.

Wilson, William G. *Alcoholics Anonymous (Third Edition).* New York: Alcoholics Anonymous World Services, 1973.

—*Alcoholics Anonymous Comes of Age.* New York: Alcoholics Anonymous World Services, 1957.

—*Twelve Steps and Twelve Traditions.* New York: Alcoholics Anonymous World Services, 1953.

Wilson Schaef, Anne. *Co-Dependence: Mistreated-Misunderstood.* San Francisco: Harper and Row, 1986.

Wiseman, Jacqueline P. *Stations of the Lost.* Englewood Cliffs, NJ: Prentice-Hall, 1970.

Woititz, Janet G. *Adult Children of Alcoholics.* Hollywood, FL: Health Communications, 1983.

Index

Lewis, Dioclesian . . . 16
Liljegren, Steven . . . 107
LSD . . . 60, 61
Lutheran Ministerium of Pennsylvania . . .
    37
Mann, Marty . . . 59, 84, 89–91
Marijuana Anonymous . . . 67, 68
Marlatt, G. Alan . . . 5, 99
Martha Washington Society . . . 14, 16
Masters, Leonard . . . 143
Mathews Larsen, Joan . . . 99
McCoy, William . . . 24
McKinley, Edward . . . 24
Medical Association for the Study of
    Inebriety and Narcotics . . . 19, 27, 53
Meyers, Robert J. . . . 5
Miller, William R. . . . 5, 99, 120–123,
    125, 140
Moderate Drinking Therapies . . . 124–128
Moderation Management . . . 135–137
Morantz, Paul . . . 80
Motivational Enhancement . . . 122, 123,
    144
Mott, John . . . 37, 39
Mount Airy Seminary . . . 37, 38
Murphy, Stacia . . . 137
Mystery of Moral Re-Armament . . . 41
Napa Valley . . . 22
Narcotics Anonymous (NA) . . . 65,
    67, 68, 143, 144
    Membership . . . 68
Nation, Carry . . . 20
National Commission on Law Observance
    and Performance . . . 25
National Council on Alcoholism and Drug
    Dependence (NCADD) . . . 84, 89, 91,
    92, 108, 137, 145
National Council for Education on
    Alcoholism (NCEA) . . . 59, 84, 89–91
National Institute on Alcohol Abuse and
    Alcoholism (NIAAA) . . . 5, 92, 101
National Longitudinal Alcoholism
    Epidemiological Survey (NLAES) . . .
    6, 101, 126, 140
National Prohibition Bureau . . . 22, 24, 26
National Society for the Salvation of
    China . . . 40
National Treatment Center Study
    Summary Report . . . 5, 93, 121
Natural History of Alcoholism Revisited
    . . . 99, 119, 140

New York Olive Plant . . . 16
New York State Inebriate Asylum . . . 19
New York World-Telegram . . . 45, 46, 54
Newton, James . . . 44
Nobleman, Susan . . . 109
North American Association of
    Alcoholism Programs . . . 91
Ohl, J.F. . . . 39
Osmond, Humphrey . . . 60
Oxford, England . . . 43
Oxford Group Movement / Moral Re-
    Armament . . . 2, 29, 37, 44–49,
    52–57, 63, 64
    Five Cs . . . 41, 56
    Four Absolutes . . . 41, 56, 57
Oxford Movement . . . 44
Parkside Medical Corporation . . . 98
Peele, Stanton . . . 66, 68, 76–78, 123
Penn-Lewis, Jessie . . . 38
Pennsylvania State College . . . 39, 40
People's Temple . . . 76
Philadelphia Society of Princeton . . . 42
Philanthropist . . . 13
Princeton University . . . 42
Prohibition . . . 1, 17–27
Prohibition Party . . . 17, 18
Psychotherapy . . . 32–35, 121–123, 140
Quarterly Journal of Studies on Alcohol
    (QJSA) . . . 84, 88
Rader, Nancy . . . 70
Ragge, Ken . . . 76, 77
Rational Recovery . . . 129, 133, 134
Rational Emotive Behavior Therapy . . .
    129, 134
Reader's Guide to Periodical Literature
    . . . 64
Real AA . . . 76, 77
Remus, George . . . 24, 25
Research Council on Problems of Alcohol
    . . . 83, 84
Resisting 12-Step Coercion . . . 123
Robertson, Nan . . . 52, 59, 60
Rogers, Carl . . . 34
Rogers, Will . . . 26
Room, Robin . . . 65
Roosevelt, Franklin . . . 26, 46
Rush, Benjamin . . . 11–13, 27
Russell, Howard . . . 18
Salvation Army . . . 1, 29–32, 53
    Nine Steps . . . 31
Sanchez-Craig, Martha . . . 126–128